BATTLE
WINNING
Tanks, Aircraft & Warships
of World War II

BATTLE WINNING
Tanks, Aircraft & Warships
of World War II

DAVID MILLER

MBI Publishing Company

This edition first published in 2000 by MBI Publishing Company,
729 Prospect Avenue, PO Box 1, Osceola, WI 54020-0001 USA

MBI Publishing Company books are also available at discounts in bulk quantity for industrial or sales-promotional use. For details write to Special Sales Manager at Motorbooks International Wholesalers & Distributors, 729 Prospect Avenue, PO Box 1, Osceola, WI 54020-0001 USA.

Library of Congress Cataloging-in-Publication Data Available

ISBN 0-7603-0968-X

Printed in Italy

THE AUTHOR

David Miller is a highly respected author of more than 35 internationally successful books on weapons and warfare. A former British Army officer, with extensive service in Europe, the Falklands, and the Far East, he was a staff journalist on the prestigious *International Defense Review*, was Editor of *Jane's Major Surface Warships*, and has contributed to many specialist defense journals.

CREDITS

Project Manager: Ray Bonds
Designed by Megra Mitchell
  Mitchell Strange Design
Color reproduction by Studio Technology

CONTENTS

INTRODUCTION

This book features a selection of important land, sea and air weapons and equipment that in my opinion can be regarded as "battle-winners" of World War II. Some of the battles described are specific, audacious and explosive engagements;, others, like the Battle of the Atlantic, could more properly be called "campaigns" whose ebb and flow witnessed successes and failures occurring over months or even years. Some of the weapons included might even be considered "war-winners", while I am sure that there are weapons that are not included which from some readers' perspectives could be classed as "battle-winners".

So what is a battle-winner? In war there are short-lived moments of glory during battles between giants, such as when the German battleship *Bismarck* sank the British battlecruiser *Hood*, in an engagement lasting barely 15 minutes, or the surprise Japanese air attack on Pearl Harbor which lasted for about two hours. Most of the time, however, war is simply a matter of keeping going; for example, the Allied bomber crews, USAAF by day and RAF by night, who went out on one raid after another until either they were shot down or their current tour of duty was up. Similarly, the British and Canadian corvette crews sailed the Atlantic for weeks on end, while their enemy the U-boatmen under the surface undertook voyages lasting up to a hundred days. Ashore, there were the

German infantrymen flogging their way across the Russian wintry steppes for months at a time, the weather and temperature often more dangerous enemies than the Soviet soldiers. For such people, their war was, for most of the time, simply a matter of endurance, interspersed with brief and violent moments of conflict and terror, when the men with the best or most imaginative plan – or, perhaps, simply the crew that was more alert and fired first – would win.

Some battle-winning weapons frequently enjoyed only a limited period of success before the enemy devised an antidote. Thus, for example, the German Junkers Ju 87 dive-bomber was an outstanding success in the campaigns of 1939-1940 when its direct attack and howling siren struck terror into the minds of its opponents, but then it was realised that it could not protect itself in the face of fighters and its day was over. Similarly, the US M3 Grant/Lee tank enjoyed only a brief success in the Western Desert, but that was enough to tide the Eighth Army over until even better tanks came along.

One lesson to be learned is how battles are often lost as a terrible consequence of underestimating the enemy. In 1939-41 Western powers regarded Japanese military equipment and the people who used it with supercilious scorn. As a result, the excellence of the "Zero" fighter came as a complete

surprise, even though reports from Western observers in China in the late 1930s had been describing it for several years. Such reports were disregarded and the cost was paid in the skies over Pearl Harbor, Manila and Malaya in December 1941 and early 1942. Similarly, the Germans considered the Russians and their equipment to be inferior in every respect, and then found themselves facing tanks and aircraft which were superior to anything in the Nazi armoury.

Perhaps the most important conclusion to be derived from the theme of this book is that whatever the quality of the equipment – whether good or bad – it is still the people that matter, the strategists and tacticians who direct its use and the operators who actually control it. The British battleship *Duke of York* was well-handled and was a winner in its meeting with the German battlecruiser *Scharnhorst*, whereas an identical ship, *Prince of Wales*, was sunk in the space of an hour by Japanese aircraft, because it was caught without air cover. Conversely, outmoded or apparently unsuitable equipment can still win if used with imagination and skill. The British Swordfish, for example, a grotesquely out-of-date biplane, was able to wreak havoc on the Italian fleet at Taranto, while the tiny, Italian-operated "human torpedo" achieved similar results against the British fleet in Alexandria harbour only a year later. Similarly, the use of B-25 Mitchell bombers from an

aircraft carrier to raid mainland Japan was something so totally unexpected and so far beyond normal military practice that the raid succeeded and had an impact out of all proportion to the resources involved and the material damage inflicted.

On consideration, few weapons can be classified as battle-winners solely in their own right. How successful, for example, would the carrier-borne fighters and fighter-bombers which took part in the Pacific campaigns have been without the mighty aircraft carriers? However, together with all their supporting elements, they contributed massively to the winning of battles. Even fewer weapons could be considered warwinners, but the contribution of some of them to the winning of battles may ultimately have led to the winning of the war, while yet others that won battles found themselves, finally, on the losing side in the war.

DAVID MILLER

CONVENTIONS USED IN THIS BOOK
Where times are given, these are all local times at the place of battle.
Where weights/displacements are given in tons, these are English tons; ie, 1 ton = 2,240lb (1,016kg); for US tons, multiply by 1.12.
Measurements are generally given to one decimal place.

BATTLE-WINNING TANKS

The tank was invented in World War I by the British for one specific purpose; to enable the infantry to break the deadlock on the Western Front by penetrating the enemy trench lines and restoring mobile warfare for the Allied infantry and cavalry. Tanks first went into action in 1916 and it took some time before methods of handling such a novel weapon were devised, the first proper use of massed tanks being at the Battle of Cambrai in 1917. However, a few imaginative men realised that the tank had the potential to be a warwinning weapon in its own right and in the 1920s and 1930s considerable efforts were devoted to development work in Germany, Great Britain, the Soviet Union and the United States, and, albeit to a lesser extent, in France. Such work concerned not only the performance and capability of the tanks, but also the more difficult problems of command and control. Thus, the British assembled the Experimental Mechanised Force in 1927 and within 10 years several other armies had created similar new armoured formations.

The most successful of these new formations were the German *panzer* divisions which played a decisive role in the *blitzkrieg* successes in Poland in 1939 and in France in 1940. These attacks were led by *panzer* units, working in close conjunction with Ju 87 Stuka dive-bombers. Their successes gained for the Germans a reputation of invincibility. Although their tanks were by no means better than the best British and French tanks, their organisation was infinitely superior. Following these victories, all major armies rapidly expanded their armoured forces, and devised new and more effective ways of handling them.

Hand-in-hand with this tactical work went the technical development of tanks, weapons and the means of production. At the start of the war the calibre of guns was 37mm on the German side in 1939 and 40mm on the British side, but this rapidly increased to the 88mm of the German tanks and the 122mm of the Soviet Stalin tanks. Similar efforts were devoted to improving the effects of the anti-tank rounds, so that armoured protection also had to be improved, and the simple vertical plates riveted together to protect most tanks in 1939 rapidly changed to much thicker armoured plate either in sections welded together or in castings, the whole forming complex shapes intended to defeat the ever more powerful anti-tank rounds.

FRANCE

The French ended World War I with a small but effective tank force, but thereafter attention was concentrated on the infantry and on the fixed defences of the Maginot Line, the armoured force running a very poor third. In general, the French followed the same line as the British, dividing tanks into reconnaissance, infantry support and medium. In 1940 they wasted their tanks in small packets, although when they were used with determination and drive they were as good as anything on the German side. One particular and persistent shortcoming of French tank design, however, was that they insisted they had one-man turrets, the same man combining the roles of commander, gunner and loader, which ensured that he performed none of them well.

GERMANY

Germany started World War II with, among others, the PzKpfw III and IV tanks which were excellent for the *blitzkrieg* tactics, but whose qualities were not quite as good as they appeared at the time and, as the Germans discovered in 1941, were certainly inferior to those of the Soviet T-34. As a result the Germans produced two rush programmes: the Panther and Tiger, which were both very effective tanks provided that they were employed properly, especially the smaller and more nimble Panther. Indeed, tank-for-tank, they were probably superior to anything the Allies ever produced, but they could never be produced or manned in the numbers required.

ITALY AND JAPAN

Two other armies, those of Italy and Japan, produced their own tank designs, but the machines were of inferior design and were seldom employed with skill. As a result, none of them ever proved to be a battlewinner.

SOVIET UNION

The Germans considered that everything about the Russians – their way of life, their methods of waging war and their military equipment – was inferior to theirs. As a result, the excellence of the Soviet KV1, T-34 and (later) the IS-2 tanks came as a complete shock. Throughout the war Soviet tanks were well armed, well protected, fast, easy-to-maintain and reliable, and collectively played a large part in the victories on the Eastern front.

UNITED KINGDOM

The British started the war with three types of tank: "light" used for reconnaissance; "infantry" which were heavy and slow, and intended to give direct support to the infantry; and "cruiser" which were dashing and fast, and intended for anti-tank battles and for the armoured breakthrough. After the 1940 campaign in France, British tanks were generally perceived as technically inferior to German tanks, although later studies have shown that on the few occasions they had been properly handled they had done as well, and that the shortcomings were in command and control rather than in actual performance. Thereafter, the British continued their own tank development, culminating in the very successful Churchill and Comet, but they also used large numbers of US tanks.

UNITED STATES

By the time the USA entered the shooting the war until December 1941 the tanks it built had already seen action with the British in the Western Desert. The Grant/Lee medium tank was effective when first deployed but it was its successor, the Sherman, which proved to be the real battlewinner. The Sherman was a good tank, although on a one-to-one basis it had neither the firepower nor protection of the German Panther. It was, however, produced in vast numbers for use by the US Army and its Allies and it was those sheer numbers that overcame the Germans.

TANK BATTLEFIELDS

Tanks were used in almost every theatre of war between 1939 and 1945, but on different scales and with varying degrees of success. As already mentioned, the early use of *blitzkrieg*, in which the *panzer* divisions played the predominant role, enabled the Germans to overrun Poland and France very quickly and at comparatively low cost. After an initial success, the same techniques were not so successful in the Western Desert, where the British gradually gained the upper hand and then, in combination with the Allied forces approaching from the west, forced the Axis armies out of North Africa.

On the other side of the world, the United States Army and Marine Corps used small numbers of tanks to great effect in the Pacific campaign, but the jungle vegetation, rugged terrain and size of the islands restricted the numbers that could be used. Tanks were, therefore, seldom able to operate independently, being normally used to support the infantry.

When the Allies landed in northern and southern France in 1944, they were able to use large armoured formations to fight their way into Germany, although German resistance was always strong and determined. The greatest tank battles of the war were, however, fought on the Eastern Front, where the vast expanses enabled huge armoured forces to be deployed in confrontations such as Kharkov (14 March 1943) and at the largest tank battle in history, Kursk (5-16 July 1943). On the German side this involved 17 *panzer* divisions, three *panzergrenadier* (armoured infantry) divisions and 16 infantry divisions, while the Soviets deployed 11 armies (each equivalent to a German corps). The Germans were decisively defeated, losing no fewer than 70,000 men and 3,000 tanks; the Soviets suffered slightly less, but could afford such losses, which the Germans could not.

During World War II tanks became steadily larger, better armed and better protected, but this was achieved at the cost of a considerable increase in weight. On the German side, for example, the PzKpfw IV (1939) weighed 19.4 tons (19,700kg), while the Panther (1943) weighed 44 tons (44,800kg) and the Tiger II (1945) 68.3 tons (69,400kg). When employed in open country such huge increases were partially offset by a dramatic growth in engine power and much improved track design, but Germany's later tanks became increasingly difficult to move along roads, especially when crossing bridges, and to transport them by train, when their width became a crucial factor.

CHAR S-35*

SPECIFICATIONS

COUTRY OF ORIGIN: France.
TYPE: medium tank.
IN SERVICE: 1936–1945.
COMBAT WEIGHT: 44,200lb (20,048kg).
DIMENSIONS: length 17.9ft(5.5m); width 6.93t (2.1m); height 8.80ft (2.7m).
ENGINE: SOMUA water-cooled eight-cylinder petrol engine, 190hp at 2,000rpm.
PERFORMANCE: road speed 23mph (37km/h); range 160 miles (257km); trench 7.8ft (2.3m); gradient 65 per cent.
GROUND PRESSURE: 13.1lb/sq in (0.9kg/sq cm).
POWER-TO-WEIGHT ratio: 10hp/ton.
ARMOUR: hull – 1.6in (41mm); turret – 2.2in (56mm) maximum.
WEAPONS: 1 x 47mm SA 35 main gun; 1 x 7.5mm coaxial MG.
AMMUNITION: 118 rounds 47mm; 1,250 rounds 7.5mm.
CREW: three.

DESIGN HISTORY

In the early 1930s the French cavalry issued a requirement for a tank to be called the *Automitrailleuse de Combat* (AMC) and a vehicle to meet this requirement was produced by the SOMUA factory. After trials this was accepted for service as the standard medium tank of the French Army, under the designation *Char S-35*. It entered service in 1936 and by the time of the capitulation of France (25 June 1940) some 500 had been manufactured.

The S-35's hull was constructed in three castings (hull floor, front superstructure and rear superstructure) which were then bolted together. The driver sat at the left front of the vehicle with the radio operator to his right, both men entering and leaving the tank via a door in the side, although an under-

BELOW: *The Char S-35 was a good tank but one of its shortcomings, shared with other French 1930s tanks, was the small turret, in which one man had to command the tank and operate the gun.*

floor escape hatch was available for emergency use. The turret, which had electric traverse, was also of cast construction, with a maximum thickness of 2.2in (56mm).

Main armament was the 47mm SA 35 gun which fired either high-explosive or armour-piercing rounds. The engine and transmission were at the rear and were separated from the fighting compartment by a fireproof bulkhead.

For its day the *Char S-35* was an excellent tank, having good armour and a 47mm gun which was more powerful that the 37mm gun fitted to PzKpfw III.

It also had some disadvantages. The three piece construction system made for ease of manufacture, but a hit on one of the joins was likely to split the tank wide open, while the small turret meant that one man had to combine the roles of commander, loader and gunner. Finally, there was a general shortage of radios and during the brief campaign some 80 percent of French tanks did not have them, which naturally made command and control very difficult.

---

* Char S-35 = Char SOMUA-35. Char = tank. SOMUA = Societé d'Outillage Mécanique et d'Usinage d'Artillerie; 35 = year of service (1935).

ABOVE: *The hull was constructed from three castings, bolted together.*

CRÉCY-SUR-SERRE: 19 MAY 1940.

At the time of the German attack in 1940 most French tanks were organised into 13 tank battalions in four Divisions *Cuirassées de Réserve* (= Reserve Cavalry Divisions (DCR); each battalion had 34 tanks and two battalions were usually grouped to form a demi-brigade. In the shambles following the first German attacks, Colonel De Gaulle, who had long been an advocate of armoured warfare, was appointed commander of 4th Armoured Division (11 May), although this formation was very short of equipment and morale was poor. Nevertheless, De Gaulle's drive and enthusiasm enabled him to lead an attack on the German lines-of-communication at Montcornet on 17 May, but this was seriously disrupted by attacks from ubiquitous Ju-57 Stukas which were called up by radio by the German ground troops as and when required.

De Gaulle's next attack was against the bridge at Crécy-sur-Serre on 19 May. By this time he had received reinforcements, particularly of artillery and tanks, the latter including two companies (40 tanks) of Char S-35. The 4th Armoured Division reached the bridge, but there was yet another example of the ineptness which characterised the whole French campaign. Arrangements had been made for French fighters to provide air cover for 4th Armoured Division against attack by Stukas, but when the time of the attack (H-hour) was brought forward someone omitted to tell the air force so that the tanks were again heavily attacked by Stukas. Then, when the French tanks had been forced to withdraw, the French fighters arrived to find both ground and air empty.

In this last battle the Char S-35 proved itself to be superior to the German PzKpfw III and IV in almost all respects, and if

deployed and directed correctly by commanders and crews with greater faith in its capabilities (and in themselves), it could have turned the tide on several occasions. As it is, however, the Char S-35 is best described as almost a battle winner, since it was so much better than the German tanks facing it and if handled better it might have had a significant effect on the battles in the summer of 1940.

ABOVE: *De Gaulle used the S-35 to overcome German tanks of 1939/40, but one man just wasn't enough.*

PzKpfw III Ausf E*

SPECIFICATIONS

COUNTRY OF ORIGIN: Germany.
TYPE: battle tank.
IN SERVICE: 1938–1945.
COMBAT WEIGHT: 42,769lb (19,400kg).
DIMENSIONS: length 17.7ft (5.4m); width 9.5ft (2.9m); height 8.0ft (2.4m).
ENGINE: Maybach HL 120 TRM water-cooled, in-line, petrol engine, 300hp at 3,000rpm.
PERFORMANCE: road speed 25mph (40km/h); cross-country speed 11mph (18km/h); range 109 miles (175km); trench 7.5ft (2.3m); gradient 30 degrees.
GROUND PRESSURE: 13.5lb/sq in (0.97kg/sq cm).
POWER-TO-WEIGHT ratio: 15.7hp/ton.
ARMOUR: 1.2in (30mm) minimum; 3.5in (90mm) maximum.
WEAPONS: 1 x 50mm KwK 39 L/42 main gun; 1 x 7.92mm MG 34 coaxial MG; 1 x 7.92mm MG 34 in hull.
CREW: five.

DESIGN HISTORY

Design work on the PzKpfw III started in 1935 with the aim of producing a tank armed with a high velocity gun whose primary mission would be to attack and eliminate other tanks. Thus, the original intention was to arm it with a 50mm gun, but it was then decided to install the 37mm, instead, since this was the calibre already used by the infantry anti-tank gun; the turret ring for the 50mm gun was retained, however. The operational requirement stipulated a combat weight of 14.76 tons (15,000kg) but, as is usual in tank designs, this was exceeded by a wide margin. The prototypes appeared in 1937 and small development batches (*Ausführung A-D*) were built, but the production order, placed in 1939, was for the *Ausführung E*, which was destined to become the standard battle tank of the German Army: 98 were in service in the Polish campaign, increasing to 350 in the attack on France.

The PzKpw III had a five-man crew, consisting of commander, gunner, loader, driver and bow machine gunner, and was well laid out, with adequate space for each man to do his job. One innovation was that the commander's position was in a "dustbin" at the rear of the turret, which gave him an excellent view. By 1940 standards the Maybach engine was satisfactory and the performance of the tank, both on roads and cross-country, was better than most contemporary tanks. The 37mm gun and the tank's armoured protection were sufficient for the Polish campaign, but proved less so in the Battle of France.

* PzKpfw III Ausf E = *Panzer Kampfwagen Drei Ausführung E* = Armoured Fighting Vehicle, Type Three, Sub-type E.

ABOVE AND RIGHT: *In combination with PzKpfw IV, the PzKpfw III spearheaded the great German advances of 1939 and 1940, when German panzers rampaged across western Europe. PzKpfw III had a five-man crew and was well laid out. Main weapon was a 37mm gun, with a 7.92mm coaxial MG and a second 7.92mm MG in the hull on the right of the driver.*

INVASION OF POLAND: SEPTEMBER – OCTOBER 1939

The Polish campaign lasted from 1 September until 5 October, 1939, and was carried out by 60 divisions of the German Army, which included nine armoured divisions, most of them equipped with PzKpfw I, II and early versions of the PzKpfw III, but with 98 of the very latest PzKpfw III *Ausführung E*. The Polish terrain was flat, with few significant obstacles; the weather was dry and not too warm – ideal conditions for tanks. In addition, the Polish army had no anti-tank capability whatsoever. All this combined to make the task of Germany's armoured forces relatively easy. The panzer divisions advanced rapidly, with the main armoured thrust being carried out by von Reichenau's Tenth Army, which moved towards Warsaw from the south-west, making its first attempt to enter the city on 8 September. It was initially pushed back, but by this stage in the brief campaign the Polish land forces had been forced into a number of pockets, while both the Navy and the Army had been eliminated in the first week. It was not that the Poles were lacking in courage – indeed, so great was their determination and so dire their equipment, that on at least one occasion Polish cavalry on horseback charged German armoured units – but they were outgeneralled and outpaced, and unable to counter the German panzer forces. Nor, it must be added, were the Poles' problems made any the easier by the perfidious attack from the east by the Soviet Union on 17 September. Thus, the pockets of resistance were eliminated one-by-one until resistance ceased on 5 October.

The PzKpfw III served in many other campaigns from 1940–1945 but never again would it be the master of the battlefield in the way it was in the Polish campaign, when the Polish Army simply had nothing to counter it.

ABOVE RIGHT: *The PzKpfw III served in many other campaigns up to 1945, but never again would it be the master of the battlefield the way it was in Poland.*

RIGHT: *PzKpfw III was one of the best tanks of the mid-late 1930s and was vastly superior to anything available to the Polish Army in their disastrous 1939 campaign. In 1941, however, Operation Barbarossa showed that it was totally outclassed by the Soviet T-34 and KV-1.*

PzKpfw IV Ausf D*

SPECIFICATIONS

COUNTRY OF ORIGIN: Germany.
TYPE: battle tank.
IN SERVICE: 1938–1945.
COMBAT WEIGHT: 43,431lb (19,700kg).
DIMENSIONS: length 19.4ft (5.9m); width 9.6ft (2.9m); height 8.5ft (2.6m).
ENGINE: Maybach HL 120 TRM V-12 water-cooled in-line petrol engine, 300hp at 3,000rpm.
PERFORMANCE: road speed 25mph (40km/h); cross-country speed 13mph (20km/h); range 125 miles (200km); trench 7.5ft (2.3m); gradient 30 degrees.
GROUND PRESSURE: 10.6lb/sq in (0.75kg/ sq cm).
POWER-TO-WEIGHT ratio: 15.5hp/ton.
ARMOUR: 0.8in (20mm) minimum; 3.5in (90mm) maximum.
WEAPONS: 1 x 75mm KwK 39 L/24 main gun; 1 x 7.92mm MG 34 coaxial MG; 1 x 7.92mm MG 34 in hull.
AMMUNITION: 75mm – 80 rounds; 7.92mm – 2,800 rounds.
CREW: five.

DESIGN HISTORY

The German Army's 1935 specifications called for two tank designs, the first, for an anti-tank vehicle, being met by the PzKpfw III, while the second, for a support tank with a large-caliber gun, was met by the PzKpfw IV. This resulted in a tank that was generally very similar to the PzKpfw III with a five-man crew in a lightly armoured hull and turret, but was slightly larger and armed with a short-barrelled 75mm gun. The PzKfw IV had an electrically traversed turret, whereas that in the PzKpfw III was hand-driven.

The engine, which was the same as that in the PzKpfw III, was at the rear with a long propeller shaft driving a front-mounted gear-box which powered the drive sprockets, also at the front. The suspension consisted of four coupled bogies on each side, sprung by leaf springs. There was a rear idler and there were four small return rollers. As with the PzKpfw III, various prototypes were built and tested, and it was the *Ausführung D* that was eventually placed in production in early 1939.

* PzKpfw IV Ausf D = Panzer Kampfwagen Vier Ausführung D = Armoured Fighting Vehicle, Type Four, Sub-type D.

LEFT AND BELOW: *PzKpfw IV with its long-barrelled L/48 75mm gun was successful in 1939-42, but by 1944 it had been* outclassed. Note the extra armour around the turret (below) which was added to increase protection, but with little effect.

INVASION OF FRANCE: 10 MAY TO 25 JUNE 1940.

Small numbers of the PzKpfw IV took part in the Polish campaign but it really came into its own in the Battle of France. The German attack in the west was conducted by some 2,500,000 German troops, with Hitler in overall command and General Brauchitsch directing the battle, which was conducted by 136 divisions, organised into three army groups, which (from north to south) were: Army Group B (Bock); Army Group A (Rundstedt); and Army Group C (Leeb). The key element in this campaign were the ten panzer divisions, with a strength of approximately 2,400 tanks, of which 1,400 (58 per cent) were the outdated and weakly armed PzKpfw I and II, while 350 were PzKpfw III and 280 the PzKpfw IV. Significant support came from 3,500 *Luftwaffe* aircraft in two *Luftflotte* (= air fleets).

The fighting started on 19 May with glider-borne and paratroop attacks against Belgian targets, while Army Groups A and B crossed the Belgian and Dutch borders at dawn, with the main weight of the attack coming through the supposedly "impassable" Ardennes. The panzer divisions swept forward, brushing aside French reconnaissance troops and crossing the River Meuse in several places on 13 May. They then headed west on a five-mile wide front, supported by the Stuka dive-bombers and introducing a new word to the international military lexicon – *blitzkrieg* (= lightning war).

The French and British did manage to carry out a few armoured counter-attacks which achieved some limited and short-lived local succ-esses, but the German advance proved irresistible, and the armoured corps soon reached the English Channel at Boulogne. The Belgians surrendered on 25 May and the British evacuated their Expeditionary Force (and some 112,00 French and Belgians) from Dunkirk. The Germans then concentrated on the final defeat of the French, which was achieved with a capitulation signed on 21 June and which came into effect on 25 June 1940.

The tanks used by the German Army in the Battle of France neither outnumbered the Anglo-French armoured forces, nor were they inherently better designs. What made the difference was that the panzer forces were simply better directed and led by inspiring generals, while individual tanks were handled by skilled and enthusiastic crews. At the vanguard of those forces was the new PzKpfw IV.

ABOVE: *PzKpfw IV, distinguishable from the PzKpfw III by (among other features) having eight bogie wheels rather than six, and four return rollers, rather than three. It was vulnerable at the sides and rear of hull and turret.*

LEFT: *An elderly Soviet couple return home, apparently oblivious to the wrecked German tank. This is a late model PzKpfw IV, whose extra protective plating has proved insufficient; note the large sheet covering part of the suspension and the spaced armour around the turret.*

PzKpfw V Panther Ausf G*

DESIGN HISTORY

At the beginning of the war, the PzKpfw IV had seemed more than adequate for the German Army's foreseeable needs, but when the Soviet T-34 was first encountered in battle in October 1941 it became clear that something much better was needed. The T-34's sloped armour, speed and manoeuverability out-dated existing German tanks at a stroke and a new operational requirement was rapidly prepared and issued in January 1942, which, in essence, simply restated the design parameters of the T-34. Indeed, consideration was even given to simply copying the T-34, but this was ruled out as being a humiliating admission of engineering inferiority. So urgent was the need that the first designs were ready in April 1942, the first prototypes were running in September and the first production machines left the M.A.N. line in January 1943.

The Panther hull had a large, single-piece glacis plate, which was well sloped. The turret was also well-sloped, with a massive mantlet with tiny apertures for the coaxial machine gun and the gunner's binocular sight. The suspension used

---

* PzKpfw V Ausf D = Panzer Kampfwagen Fünf Ausführung G = Armoured Fighting Vehicle, Type Five, Sub-type G.

SPECIFICATIONS

COUNTRY OF ORIGIN: Germany.
TYPE: battle tank.
IN SERVICE: 1943–1945.
COMBAT WEIGHT: 98,766lb (44,800kg).
DIMENSIONS: length 22.5ft (6.7m); width 10.8ft (3.3m); height 9.7ft (3.0m).
ENGINE: Maybach HL 230 P 30 V-12 water-cooled in-line petrol engine, 700hp at 3,000rpm.
PERFORMANCE: road speed 29mph (46km/h); cross-country speed 15mph (24km/h); range 110 miles (177km); trench 3.0ft (0.9m); gradient 30 degrees.
GROUND PRESSURE: 12.5lb/sq in (0.88kg/sq cm).
POWER-TO-WEIGHT ratio: 15.9hp/ton.
ARMOUR: 0.6in (20mm) minimum; 4.7in (120mm) maximum.
WEAPONS: 1 x 75mm KwK 42 2L/70 main gun; 1 x 7.92mm MG 34 coaxial MG; 1 x 7.92mm MG 34 in hull.
AMMUNITION: 75mm – 82 rounds.
CREW: five.

interleaved bogies sprung on torsion-bars, a system which had been in service for some time on German half-tracks and on the Tiger I. The springs were torsion bars mounted transversely inside the tank (unlike the Porsche design) but, in an innovation, were shaped like a hair-pin, to give double the length. Steering was by an adaption of the British Merritt-Brown system, with hydraulically operated disc brakes and epicyclic gears to each track, which

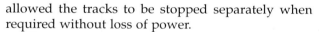

LEFT AND BELOW: *The PzKpfw V Panther was very heavy by the standards of the day, but its powerful engine gave it a healthy 16hp/ton power:weight ratio. The main gun was a long-barrel (70-calibre) 75mm with an exceptionally high muzzle velocity. In a one-to-one engagement the Panther could defeat almost any Allied tank, but was overcome by sheer numbers.*

allowed the tracks to be stopped separately when required without loss of power.

The turret was designed by Rheinmetall-Borsig and mounted a 75mm 70-calibre gun, which had an exceptionally high muzzle velocity of 3,070ft/sec (936m/s), making it very accurate and giving it a very good first-round hit probability. This gun could penetrate 4.7in (120mm) of sloped plate at 1,090yd (1,000m) and this, together with the protection of the frontal armour, meant that the Panther could stand-off from Allied tanks, even the T-34 and KV-1, and knock them out without being harmed itself. Indeed, the US Army calculated that it required five Shermans to knock out one Panther. The one tank normally impervious to the Panther's 75mm was the Soviet IS-2, but this did not reach service until 1944.

The transmission system was somewhat curious in that the rear-mounted engine drove a front-mounted gear-box/steering unit via a long transmission shaft which ran the full length of the

LEFT : *The PzKpfw V Panther was a brilliant design with a massive, sloped glacis plate and a 75mm gun mounted in a thick mantlet. This picture shows the almost total absence of vertical surfaces, the angling greatly increasing protection against incoming anti-tank rounds.*

BELOW: *This side view of a PzKpfw V Panther shows the interleaved roadwheels, which gave a good ride, but were liable to freeze in Russian winter, a fact noticed early by the Soviet Army, which was quick to take advantage of the German tank crews' problems.*

inside of the tank (and thus forced the turret to be higher than would otherwise have been the case). Short transverse shafts then took the drive to the front sprocket final drives. The main reason that the German designers liked this system was that they believed it was preferable for the track to arrive at the drive sprocket clear of mud, which was only possible with forward drive.

One anomalous feature of the Panther's history is that the first model to appear was *Ausführung D*, of which the first 20 off the production line had the thinner 2.3in (60mm) glacis plate and the less powerful Maybach HL-210 engine; from the 21st onwards the thicker glacis plate and more powerful HL-230 engine were fitted. The next model to appear, in late 1943, was the *Ausführung A* which had a new cupola and a ball-mounting for the bow machine gun. It was also fitted with side skirts to protect the track and hull sidewall from shaped-charge anti-tank weapons. It was also the first tank to be coated in *"Zimmerit"* which was intended to prevent magnetic mines from sticking to the tank. The final version was *Ausführung G* which was essentially intended to incorporate various improvements to make the tank more reliable, eliminated the driver's port in the glacis, placed armoured protection around the ammunition stowage bins, and increased the number of 75mm rounds carried from 79 to 82.

ABOVE: *Confident and relaxed men of* Panzer Regiment 33 *accompany their PzKpfw V en route by rail to counter the Allied invasion, June 1944.*

RIGHT: *PzKpfw V Panthers of SS-Division Hitlerjügend (Hitler Youth) thunder through a French town in June 1944.*

Not surprisingly, there were many problems with the early versions, many of which were attributable to the late decision to increase glacis plate armour from 2.3in (60mm) to 80mm (3in), which raised the tank's weight from 34.4 to 44 tons. However, it was too late to upgrade the capabilities of components affected by such a change and many, particularly the engine and transmission, were overstressed: cooling was inadequate and engines caught fire. The wheels also gave trouble as the bolts securing the rim to the disc tended to shear, a problem compounded if the failure was on an inner wheel, since the two outer wheels then had to be removed to get at the inner one.

Over 5,000 Panthers were built, 3,740 of them in 1944 alone, the monthly production rate peaking at 155 in August 1944. Once the original problems had been resolved, the only problems with the Panther were that it was over-complicated, mechanically unreliable and expensive to produce, although it cost just under half that of a Tiger II.

ALL FRONTS: 1943-1945

The Panther was not fielded until 1943, when Hitler, always fascinated by new technology, insisted that it be used at Kursk in July 1943, which resulted in a debacle: many broke down and few survived the first day of battle, while those that were salvaged had to be sent back to the factory to be rebuilt. But, from Kursk onwards the glory days of German advances on all fronts were over and the Panther rarely participated in anything other than a local tactical success followed by a withdrawal to the next defensive position. Nevertheless, it was fought hard over the following two years of one defeat after another.

It had few shortcomings, although its suspension caused problems. The interleaved road wheels gave superb running characteristics, but the system tended to freeze-up when clogged with snow or frozen mud in the Russian winter.

The Panther did not win any battles of its own; it entered service too late for that. What it did achieve, however, was to make the Allies' victory - on both Eastern and Western fronts - much more costly than it otherwise would have been. It also set the pattern for virtually every main battle tank design over the following sixty years.

ABOVE: *End of the road for a PzKpfw V. Only Allied aircraft or guns such as the British* *17-pounder could inflict such massive damage on this well-protected tank.*

PzKpfw VI Tiger I*

SPECIFICATIONS

COUNTRY OF ORIGIN: Germany.
TYPE: battle tank.
IN SERVICE: 1942–1944.
COMBAT WEIGHT: 121,253lb (55,000kg).
DIMENSIONS: length 27.0ft (8.3m); width 12.3ft (3.7m); height 9.3ft (2.9m).
ENGINE: Maybach HL 230 P 45 V-12 water-cooled in-line petrol engine, 700hp at 3,000rpm.
PERFORMANCE: road speed 24mph (38km/h); cross-country speed 12mph (20km/h); range 62 miles (100km); trench 5.9ft (1.8m); gradient 35 degrees.
GROUND PRESSURE: 14.8lb/sq in (1.0kg/sq cm).
POWER-TO-WEIGHT ratio: 12.9hp/ton.
ARMOUR: 1.0in (25.4mm) minimum; 4.3in (110mm) maximum.
WEAPONS: 1 x 88mm KwK 36 L/36 main gun; 1 x 7.92mm MG 34 coaxial MG; 1 x 7.92mm MG 34 in hull.
AMMUNITION: 88mm – 92 rounds.
CREW: five.

DESIGN HISTORY:

By late 1941 it was clear that PzKpfw III and IV were seriously outclassed by the Soviet T-34 and KV-1. This led to an urgent operational requirement for a new battle tank armed with the 88mm high-velocity gun, in a hull and turret made of armour sufficient to defeat all existing and predicted anti-tank weapons. The Henschel design, fitted with a Krupp turret was accepted and placed in production as the PzKpfw VI Tiger. At the time, the Tiger was the most powerful tank in the world, combining its formidable 88mm gun, which could penetrate 4.4in (112mm) of armour at 492yd (450m) – more than enough to penetrate most Allied tanks of the day – with frontal armour that defeated all contemporary

* PzKpfw VI = Panzer Kampfwagen Sechs = Armoured Fighting Vehicle, Type Six.

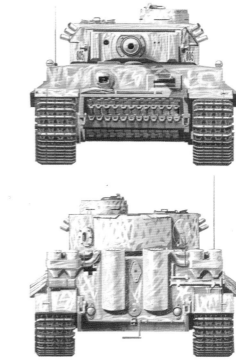

ABOVE: *At the time it appeared, PzKpfw VI Tiger I was the most powerful tank in the world, combining excellent protection with the firepower of the legendary 88mm gun, which had already proved itself as an anti-aircraft weapon and as a towed, wheeled anti-tank gun. Note also the smoke-grenade dischargers on the turret, one of the earliest examples of a device which is now used on virtually every tank. The end views show the width of this tank, 12.3ft (3.7m), which caused problems when transporting it by rail, while the weight often gave difficulties in crossing road bridges. It was, however, a formidable opponent, greatly respected by its enemies.*

projectiles. Most Tigers were deployed in 30-strong heavy tank battalions, controlled by army or corps headquarters, but some were also issued to armoured divisions, particularly in the Waffen-SS.

The Tiger had several drawbacks. The range was too limited for many operations, its top speed was low, and the weight was too great, while maintenance, particularly of the transmission system, was a nightmare. The suspension, with overlapping roadwheels gave a soft and stable ride, but was very complicated and tended to freeze-up in the Russian winter (having discovered this, the

ABOVE: *Tiger I in a Normandy orchard, summer 1944. Note the vertical glacis plate,* **Zimmerit** *coating on the hull and turret, and interleaved roadwheels. Tiger I was slow and had a short range, but its 88mm gun and excellent protection made it a fearsome fighting vehicle.*

LEFT: *A Tiger I rolls through the Normandy countryside. The gasoline drum on the rear deck was necessary because of Tiger I's notoriously short range of 62 miles (100km). Note the width of the tracks, necessary to keep the ground pressure within acceptable limits.*

Soviet Army often timed its attacks for dawn, knowing that the Tigers would probably be immobilised). The tank was too wide for rail transport in its normal configuration and had to have a special, narrower track fitted and the outer roadwheels removed, the whole tedious process having to be repeated on arrival at the railhead.

Hitler pressed for the Tiger's earliest use, as a result of which they were thrown into battle near Leningrad in the late summer of 1942, well spread-out, in small numbers and on unsuitable ground; the result was a fiasco. Once it had been properly analysed it was very effective, but, despite its undoubted strengths, the Tiger was very heavy and slow moving, and once the Allies had devised tactics to deal with it production ended and it was phased out in late 1944 after only some 1,300 had been produced.

LEFT: *A sight familiar to any military person, as an "orders group" is held in the field with battalion commander, Westernhagen (third from left in camouflage suit), briefing his company commanders while the soldiers look on, waiting for the officers to sort things out.*

BELOW: *A Tiger I crew pauses for a meal during the Normandy fighting, but not before camouflaging the tank from the ever-present enemy fighter-bombers. This gives a very clear view of the muzzlebrake, which reduced the recoil without affecting the weapon's efficiency.*

EXPLOITS OF PANZER ACE, SS-MAJOR WITTMANN

Air force fighter aces are widely acknowledged but successful tank commanders remain virtually unknown, one of the few to have achieved fame being *Waffen-SS* soldier, Michael Wittmann. As an NCO, Wittmann commanded an armoured car in the Polish and French campaigns, and an assault gun in the Balkan and the early part of the Russian campaigns. He was very successful in all of these and after he had destroyed six enemy tanks in one engagement during the Battle of Rostov in autumn 1941 he was selected for a commission and appointed to command a tank platoon in *SS Panzer Regiment I* on the Eastern Front.

Wittmann's abilities were demonstrated on the first day of the Battle of Kursk (5 July 1943) where he commanded a platoon of five Tiger I tanks in the heavy *panzer* company, which formed his division's advance guard. Wittmann's gunner, Balthasar Woll, quickly knocked out a Russian anti-tank gun and the platoon reached a Russian strong-point where it destroyed several T-34s and put a number of others to flight. Wittmann then advanced on to another Russian strong-point but was diverted to go to the aid of another tank platoon which had been surrounded by T-34s. Wittmann led his platoon as fast as the tanks would allow – probably no more than about 10mph (16km/h) – but took the Russians by surprise by arriving from their rear. Wittmann quickly destroyed three T-34s, thus enabling the other panzer platoon to break out and resume its advance. By the end of the day Wittmann's platoon had destroyed eight Russian T-34s and seven anti-tank guns.

Wittmann was an exceptional and very skilful tank commander who consistently obtained the very best out of his Tiger tanks, always employing them in an aggressive fashion.

ABOVE: *Unlike fighter pilots, few tankmen have achieved 'ace' status, exceptions being SS tank officer Michael Wittmann (left) and his gunner, Balthasar Woll (right), whose triumphs were in Tiger Is.*

LEFT: *Tiger I of Wittmann's company. Wittmann fought on both the Eastern and Western fronts. He showed an affinity for armoured warfare, being able to handle groups of* panzers *as effectively as he did his own tank. His favourite machine was the Tiger I and he was in one when he was killed in Normandy on 8 August 1944.*

PzKpfw VI Königstiger (Tiger II)*

SPECIFICATIONS

COUNTRY OF ORIGIN: Germany.

TYPE: heavy tank.

IN SERVICE: 1944–1945.

COMBAT WEIGHT: 153,000lb (69,400kg).

DIMENSIONS: length 23.8ft (7.3m); width 12.3ft (4.3m); height 10.1ft (3.3m).

ENGINE: Maybach HL 230 P 30 V-12 water-cooled in-line petrol engine, 600hp at 3,000rpm.

PERFORMANCE: road speed 24mph (38km/h); cross-country speed 11mph (17km/h); range 68 miles (110km); trench 8.1ft (2.5m); gradient 35 degrees.

GROUND PRESSURE: 15.2lb/sq in (1.1kg/sq cm).

POWER-TO-WEIGHT ratio: 8.8hp/ton.

ARMOUR: 1.6in (40mm) minimum; 7.3in (185mm) maximum.

WEAPONS: 1 x 88mm KwK 43 L/71 main gun; 1 x 7.92mm MG 34 coaxial MG; 1 x 7.92mm MG 34 in hull.

AMMUNITION: 88mm – 80 rounds.

CREW: five.

DESIGN HISTORY

The Tiger I had hardly entered service before the German General Staff requested a better successor, which would be superior in armour and hitting power to anything that the Soviet Army could produce. Two design proposals were produced, both incorporating the latest sloped armour technology and the longer, 71-caliber version of the 88mm gun. Porsche's design for the earlier Tiger I competition had been rejected and the company tried again, their bid again having electric transmission; it was again rejected. The contract went to Henschel, although Porsche had been so confident of winning that they had already manufactured 50 turrets and, as a sop to the losers, these were installed in the first 50 Henschel tanks. Thereafter Henschel fitted its own turret, which was simpler and had better protection.

RIGHT: *The mission of the Königstiger, the most powerful operational tank of World War II, was to dominate the battlefield; this monster did that,*

BELOW: *Tiger IIs drawn up in line abreast. These formidable tanks were often deployed in groups of five or less to halt or delay much larger numbers of Allied tanks.*

Tiger II was the best protected tank to enter production during the war, but this was achieved at the price of weight and it is interesting to compare it with the Soviet IS-2 which mounted a much larger gun – 122mm versus 88mm – in a tank weighing 46 tons compared to the Tiger II's 69 tons. However, the German gun had greater terminal effect, its penetrating power against homogenous armour plate at 547yd (500m) being 7in (182mm) compared to 5.5in (140mm) for the Russian gun. One problem, however, was that the high velocity projectiles caused excessive barrel wear, but later models had a two-piece barrel, enabling the faster-wearing section to be changed easily.

The Tiger II hull was welded, with acutely sloped armour, and the well-designed Henschel turret had a separate cupola for the commander, with an excellent view. In all, 485 were produced, although shortage of materials and fuel gradually slowed the production rate.

---

* PzKpfw VI Königstiger Tiger II = Panzer Kampfwagen Sechs Königstiger Tiger II = Armoured Fighting Vehicle, Type Six, King-tiger, Tiger II. (For some reason the Western Allies translated Königstiger as 'Royal Tiger.')

LEFT: *Königstigers in the West in late 1944. They are the early version with the Porsche turret, which mounted the same 88mm KwK 43 L/71 main gun, but had a rounded front and smaller mantlet than the more satisfactory Henschel version.*

BELOW: *US soldiers examine a Königstiger, which met its end at the hands of Allied fighter-bombers during the Battle of the Bulge. The figures clearly demonstrate the massive size of this vehicle.*

LEFT: *The first few days of the Battle of the Bulge were the high point in the career of the Königstiger. This one has the Henschel turret.*

RIGHT: *This picture clearly shows the aperture on the left of the glacis plate for the bow machine gun, a weapon of dubious value, which the Germans were very reluctant to discontinue.*

BELOW RIGHT: *A captured Königstiger, with the Henschel turret (note squared face, large mantlet). It was an excellent tank when used correctly, but Hitler ignored the experts' advice.*

BATTLE OF THE BULGE: DECEMBER 1944 – JANUARY 1945.

The Tiger II was supposed to dominate the battlefield, which it could do, provided the crew used it correctly. Its enormous size – it was a little over 10ft (3m) high and 12ft (3.6m) wide – made it difficult to conceal on the battlefield, although this was counteracted to a certain extent by its extraordinary degree of protection. Its great weight (68 tons) made it impossible for it to use many bridges, which restricted its mobility and this, coupled with its slow speed, meant that on several occasions it was left behind in a fast-moving battle, a fate which befell several of these tanks on both Eastern and Western fronts.

Like Tiger I, the Tiger II was too wide in its normal state for transportation by railroad; as a result it had to have the side skirts and the outer roadwheels removed and a narrower track fitted before being loaded on to a flat-car – and the whole time-consuming process had to be reversed on arrival at the destination. Nevertheless, such railroad moves were often carried out and after the Battle of the Bulge, for example, 36 Tiger IIs were moved in late January 1945 from the Aachen area to Hungary by railroad, the trains being routed via Berlin and Vienna for security reasons; the whole journey took some two weeks.

The aim of the German offensive in the Ardennes (Battle of the Bulge) was for a panzer-led attack which would strike swiftly through the Allies to reach Antwerp, thus cutting the Allied forces into two and crippling their supplies. For this operation *1st SS Panzer Division* (*Leibstandarte Adolf Hitler*) was divided into four *kampfgruppen*; in essence, temporary brigades. Kampfgruppe Peiper consisted of two *panzer* battalions (*1st SS* [38 Panther, 34 PzKpfw IV] and *501st SS* Heavy (45 Tiger II), plus one *panzergrenadier* battalion (infantry mounted in half-tracks), two engineer companies and two air defence companies, together with the usual support and logistics troops.

The *501st SS Heavy Panzer Battalion* was directly subordinate to headquarters *1st SS Panzer Corps*, but for this operation was allocated to *1st SS Panzer Division*, which, in its turn, allocated it to the spearhead, *Kampfgruppe Peiper*, commanded by one of the most famous *Waffen-SS* officers, Colonel Jochen Peiper. The *501st* was commanded by Major Hein von Westernhagen, who travelled with Peiper throughout the battle.

The attack was launched on 16 December and by 17th *KG Peiper* had reached Ligneuville, by which time some Tiger IIs had already broken down or were bogged down. By 18 December the battle for the village of Stavelot had started with at least seven Tiger IIs through the village, but most spread out far behind. One small group, including four Tiger IIs, reached Stavelot from another direction on their way to join up with *KG Peiper*, but came under fire from US troops. Three of the Tiger IIs managed to get across the bridge over the River Ambleve, but one was damaged in an air strike and totally blocked the entrance to the bridge until well after dark, when its crew finally managed to get it going again. One of those that had crossed the bridge earlier became immobilised when trying to climb over a huge pile of rubble in a side street and had to be abandoned. By this stage in the battle 27 Tiger IIs were in various states of disrepair back along route.

The battle for Stavelot continued on 19 December, with the Germans on one side of the river needing to capture the bridge in order to advance, and the Americans on the other side determined to prevent them. One German attack was launched at 1300, which included 10 tanks, a mixture of Tiger IIs and PzKpfw IVs. The assault was led by a Tiger II, but the Americans saw its barrel slowly emerging from cover and as soon as the hull appeared an M36 tank-destroyer fired a single armour-piercing round which penetrated the hull just above the track and immobilised the German tank, which then blocked the approach to the bridge for the

remainder of the battle. (The M36 was a tracked tank destroyer armed with a 3.5in/90mm high velocity gun, which, like the German "88", had originally been designed as an anti-aircraft gun.) By the end of the battle the *501st* still had 31 Tiger IIs, but 13 of these were under repair.

Von Westernhagen's Tiger IIs knocked out a number of US Shermans for relatively low losses of their own. The Tiger II was an exceptionally powerful tank and a potential battlewinner, but the Battle of the Bulge shows how badly it could be misemployed. First, although the terrain through which *KG Peiper's* attacks were launched was by no means impassable to tanks, the dense woods, narrow winding roads and numerous rivers made it by no means the best 'tank country.' Added to this, Hitler deliberately chose a time when bad weather was expected, since this would limit Allied air attacks, although, perversely, he included German air strikes in his plan. At the operational level, *KG Peiper's* task was to be the fast-moving, hard-hitting spearhead of the attack, so it seems curious that the heavy, lumbering Tiger IIs should have been included, while in a battle where the Germans were desperately short of petrol, the inclusion of such 'thirsty' tanks was a source of constant problems. Nevertheless, when used properly the Tiger II was very effective and could engage many times its own numbers of enemy and knock them all out without damage to itself.

IS-2

DESIGN HISTORY

The General Staff of the Soviet Army instigated the development of a new heavy tank in 1941. In outline, the requirement stated that the new tank was to mount an 85mm gun, to have a four-man crew, and to be immun to the German 50mm anti-tank projectiles. It was also required to be no heavier than the KV-1 and to have at least the same performance. The design bureau based its work on experience gained with the KV-series and prototypes were running in 1943. The new tank was called the Iosef Stalin (sometimes referred to as the IS-85 because of its 85mm gun) and after the three prototypes were demonstrated to the special committee of the Main Defence Commissariat the design was approved, with authority to begin mass-production being given in October 1943.

As required, the new tank weighed little more than the KV (indeed, only fractionally more than the German Panther medium tank), but had thicker and much better shaped armour, which provided excellent protection, with a new cast turret (the same turret as that fitted to KV-85) mounting an 85mm

COUNTRY OF ORIGIN: Soviet Union.
TYPE: heavy tank.
IN SERVICE: 1943–1945.
COMBAT WEIGHT: 101,963lb (46,250kg).
DIMENSIONS: length (including gun) 32.8ft (10.7m); width 10.5ft (3.4m); height 8.9ft (2.9m).
ENGINE: V-2 IS 12-cylinder, water-cooled diesel engine, 520hp at 2,000rpm.
PERFORMANCE: road speed 23mph (37km/h); range 94 miles (150km); trench 8.1ft (2.9m); gradient 70 per cent.
GROUND PRESSURE: 11.3lb/sq in (0.8kg/sq cm).
POWER-TO-WEIGHT ratio: 13.0hp/ton.
ARMOUR: 0.8in (19mm) minimum; 5.2in (132mm) maximum.
WEAPONS: 1 x 122mm M1943 (D-25) L/43 main gun; 1 x 12.7mm M1938 DshK coaxial MG; 1 x 7692mm DT or DTM MG in hull.
AMMUNITION: 122mm – 28 rounds.
CREW: four.

gun. The General Staff was still not satisfied, however, not least because the T-34 "medium" tank also mounted the 85mm gun and it was considered that a "heavy" tank should mount something more

BELOW: *An IS-2 in a Russian forest in early 1945. The D-23 122mm main gun was the most powerful tank gun to be fielded in World War II, being far more effective than the German 88mm, let alone the British 17-pounder (76.2mm) and US 75mm guns. The large muzzle-brake reduced the recoil of the gun, easing the space problems inside the cramped turret.*

powerful. As a result, a few prototypes were fitted with a new 100/54mm gun, but this tank (designated IS-100) was not placed in production because an even more powerful gun of 122mm calibre was under development. This led to the IS-2, which was running in early October 1943 and placed in production at the end of that month, with 102 completed by 31 December.

The IS-2 was, by a very wide margin, the most powerful tank to achieve combat status in World War II, its 122mm gun being far more effective than the American 75mm, the British 76.2mm (17-pounder) or German 88mm. The 122mm fired separate ammunition, the projectile weighing 55lb (25kg) with a muzzle velocity of 2,562ft/s (781m/s), and with three "natures" available: high explosive and two types of armour-piercing. Furthermore, its armoured protection was unparalleled for thickness, shaping and ballistic protection, while its diesel engine gave it a reasonable degree of mobility.

EASTERN FRONT: 1944–1945

A few early models were deployed in January 1944 in the battles around the Cherkassy Pocket, with the tank designer, General Potin, personally observing the tank in action and gaining vital information as to its performance and shortcomings. In the shorter term, the lessons he learned were rapidly incorporated into current production, while in the longer term they led to the IS-3, but this did not enter service until just after the end of the war, and is thus outside the scope of this book.

The IS-2 took part in virtually every battle from early 1944 onwards and proved itself an excellent battle tank. The Soviet designers managed to accommodate the 122mm gun, by far the largest calibre World War II tank gun, together with 28 rounds, in a vehicle weighing 45.5 tons (46.25 tonnes). By comparison, the German heavy tank, Tiger II, weighed considerably more at 68.3 tons (69.4 tonnes) with a somewhat smaller 88mm gun, which was only partially compensated for by the great number of rounds carried (80).

It should be noted that after the war the IS-2 and its slightly improved successor, the IS-3, were considered such a serious threat that the US developed the M-103 and the British the Conqueror, both armed with 120mm guns and intended solely to counter the IS-2/-3.

The IS-2 did not win any World War II battle single-handed, but it was a leading part of the Soviet armoured forces, which so decisively beat the Germans during the years 1943–1945.

KV-1

SPECIFICATIONS

COUNTRY OF ORIGIN: Soviet Union.

TYPE: heavy tank.

IN SERVICE: 1940–1945.

COMBAT WEIGHT: 104,791lb (47,500kg).

DIMENSIONS: length 20.6ft (6.3m); width 10.2ft (3.1m); height 7.9ft (2.4m).

ENGINE: V-2-K IS 12-cylinder, water-cooled diesel engine, 600hp at 2,000rpm.

PERFORMANCE: road speed 22mph (35km/h); range 156 miles (250km); trench 8.5ft (2.8m); gradient 70 per cent.

GROUND PRESSURE: 10.7lb/sq in (0.75kg/sq cm).

POWER-TO-WEIGHT ratio: 12.6hp/ton.

ARMOUR: maximum 3.0in (75mm) to 3.9in (100mm) depending on model.

WEAPONS: 1 x 76.2mm F-34 main gun; 1 x 7.62mm DT coaxial MG; 1 x 7.62mm DT MG in hull; 1 x 7.62mm DT MG in rear face of turret (some).

AMMUNITION: 76mm – 111 rounds; 7.62mm – 3,000 rounds.

CREW: five.

DESIGN HISTORY

At the outbreak of World War II the Soviet Red Army was practically the only army in the world to have a heavy tank not only in production but also in service. This was the KV-1 (Klimenti Voroshilov) which had been designed by a group of engineers at the Kirov Factory in Leningrad. Progress in the project was astonishing: design work started in February 1939, the wooden mock-up was ready for inspection in April, the first prototype was demonstrated to the General Staff in September, acceptance was completed in December, and production started in February 1940.

Following their experiences in the Spanish Civil War and in the "Manchurian Incident" (a 1939 border dispute with Japan) the Soviet General Staff had concluded, quite correctly and much earlier than its Western counterparts, that the day of the rivetted tank was over. Thus, the original KV-1 had a welded hull, although later versions had an even more effective cast hull. The main armament was the same 76mm gun that armed the T-34, which easily outranged the 37mm gun on German PzKpfw III and IV tanks and also eased logistic support, since both types of tank needed just one caliber of ammunition. There was one DT machine gun coaxial with the main gun and a second in the nose plate and to the left of the driver's position. Later KV-1s also had a machine gun mounted in the rear plate of the turret in an attempt to overcome the problem of German tank-hunting teams which managed to mount the rear of the hull, when one man would fire a sub-machine gun through a vision slit for the crew to open their hatch covers, whereupon the other Germans, waiting on the rear deck, would throw hand-grenades into the interior of the tank.

Soviet tank designers were also the first to appreciate the important tactical advantages of using diesel fuel, which ignited far less readily than did gasoline. The V-2K engine of the KV-1 was also considerably more powerful than other contemporary tank engines, but despite this, one of the KV-

LEFT AND ABOVE: *The KV-1A heavy tank was armed with various models of 76.2mm guns.*

This particular version of the tank has an additional MG in the rear of the turret, an idea which was not pursued as it served little tactical purpose. Note the very angular design of the turret compared to the more rounded cast version mounted on later KV-1s, such as those shown opposite (below).

EASTERN FRONT: 1942–1944

When the Germans attacked the Soviet Union in June 1941 the Red Army had as many as a thousand of their new KV-1 and T-34 tanks in service, but they were scattered around the vast country in small groups. Within two weeks of the invasion, however, this had been put right, as was made clear in a report from a German unit in LVI Corps (von Manstein), which reported that an enormous and apparently shot-proof tank of unknown design had suddenly appeared astride a supply route and for several hours had resisted every German attempt to destroy it. The Germans had brought an 88mm gun into use but this had been knocked out by the unknown tank's powerful gun, and eventually a major diversion had to be staged to draw the tank into an ambush, where another "88" had destroyed it at close range. This was the KV-1's first appearance in battle and during the defensive phase of the Soviet "Great Patriotic War" many such actions were fought, gradually slowing down the German advance, before new weapons and tanks could be brought into service to send the Germans back whence they came.

1's main disadvantages was that it was very slow.

There was a five-man crew. The driver sat in the centre at the front with the machine gunner/radio operator to his left, both protected by a 75mm-thick homogenous steel plate, which was reinforced in later models by a 35mm appliqué plate. The turret contained the commander (who did not have a separate cupola), gunner and loader.

ABOVE: *A convoy of KV-1s tanks drives through Leningrad on the way to the front. Soviet tank designers were first to appreciate that diesel fuel ignited far less readily than petrol/gasoline.*

BELOW: *KV-1s built with funds donated by Moscow area farmers are presented to Red Army tankmen. Such practical gestures of support took place in many countries during World War II.*

T-34

SPECIFICATIONS

COUNTRY OF ORIGIN: Soviet Union.
TYPE: battle tank.
IN SERVICE: 1940–1945.
COMBAT WEIGHT: 70,547lb (32,000kg).
DIMENSIONS: length 19.8ft (6.0m); width 9.6ft (2.9m); height 7.81ft (2.4m).
ENGINE: V-2-34 12-cylinder, water-cooled diesel engine, 500hp at 1,800rpm.
PERFORMANCE: road speed 31mph (50km/h); cross-country speed 24mph (39.km/h); range 186 miles (300km); trench 8.1ft (2.5m); gradient 65 pe rcent.
GROUND PRESSURE: 11.2lb/sq in (0.8kg/sq cm).
POWER-TO-WEIGHT ratio: 15.9hp/ton.
ARMOUR: 0.7in (18mm) minimum; 2.4in (60mm) maximum.
WEAPONS: T-34/76 – 1 x 76.2mm M1939 main gun; T-34/85 – 1 x 85mm M1944 S53 (D-5T) main gun; all – 1 x 7.62mm DT coaxial MG; all – 1 x 7.62mm DT MG in hull.
AMMUNITION: 76.2mm – 76 rounds; 85mm – 76 rounds.
CREW: four.

DESIGN HISTORY

In the 1930s, the tank design team at the Komintern Factory in Kharkov led by M. I. Koshkin produced a series of designs culminating in the T-32 with a 45mm gun, which was shown to the Soviet Armoured Directorate of the General Staff in early 1939. The directorate was happy with the general design but recommended that a more powerful gun be fitted and that thicker armour should be used for both hull and turret. Work leading to the completion of the first prototype of this revised vehicle was in progress when the deteriorating international situation led the General Staff to order the tank into immediate full production designated T-34.

The T-34 introduced shaped, cast armour which provided excellent protection for the crew, while the

RIGHT: *The T-34/76B, which has a turret made from rolled plate and welded armour, and is armed with the long barrel L/40 76.2mm gun. Note the bow machine gun and the engine exhausts on the rear. The radio antenna on the right trackguard and stowage boxes on the left trackguard indicate that this is a company commander's*

long-barrelled 76.2mm gun was the heaviest main armament used in any main battle tank at the time. Power was provided by a diesel engine, a development of the model already in use in the BT-7M tank, the diesel fuel greatly reducing the risk of fire. Of equal importance in such a vast country was the fuel economy which, coupled to the use of eight internal and four external fuel tanks, ensured a considerable range: 186 miles (300km) for the T-34, compared to 110 miles (177km) for the German Panther and a paltry 62 miles (100km) for the Tiger I.

A tank designed by the American, J. W. Christie, had been imported from the United States in 1930 and the suspension was found to be highly suitable for the type of fast-moving, long-range tank operations envisaged by the Red Army. The BT-7 was the first Soviet tank with a four-wheel Christie suspension, but this was further developed for use on the T-34, with five roadwheels on each side permitting high speeds, even across rough terrain, while the 19in (48cm) wide tracks gave a low ground pressure. In addition, the overall design of the tank not only facilitated rapid mass production but also lent itself to simple maintenance in the field.

The T-34 was upgunned on several occasions. The first version was armed with the 76.2mm M1939 gun mounted in a welded turret of rolled plate, but a new cast turret was soon introduced. During mid-1941 a new M1940 F-34 gun was adopted, still 75mm calibre, but with a longer barrel and

thus greater muzzle velocity and penetration. Then, in autumn 1943, the 85mm S-53 (D-5T) gun was adopted, which had an even better performance. With the new gun the tank was designated T-34/85 (the earlier tank being retrospectively re-designated the T-34/76) and was approved for production in December 1943; it was so successful that it remained in production in until 1955. A sad footnote to the history of the T-34 is that the head of the design team, Koshkin, died of pneumonia in September 1940 and thus did not live to see the triumphs of his great tank design.

ABOVE: *Early model T-34/76A with a welded armour turret and a 76mm gun. The suspension of this Soviet tank was based on the system developed by US engineer, JW Christie. The Soviets purchased one of his tanks in 1930 and incorporated the system into the BT-7 fast tank and then into the T-34.*

RIGHT: *In the days before the introduction of armoured personnel carriers, the Red Army frequently used its tanks to transport infantry across the battlefield. These T-34/85s are seen advancing through the Moldavian Republic after crossing the River Dniester in the summer of 1943.*

CHERKASSY POCKET: FEBRUARY 1944

The T-34 made its combat debut on 22 June 1941 in the vicinity of Grodno in Byelorussia, where it came as a complete surprise to the Germans as it rendered their then standard tanks – the PzKpfw III and IV – obsolete at a stroke. The German Army quickly learnt to treat it with the greatest respect; indeed, consideration was even given to placing a reverse-engineered copy into production in Germany, but this was turned down on political grounds, although the troops on the Eastern Front had no such qualms and many captured T-34s were pressed into service with German panzer units.

In January 1944 the Soviet Army was slowly pushing Field Marshal von Manstein and his German Army Group South out of the Ukraine and at one point found themselves with a large group of German troops pinned into a triangular-shaped salient, which the Soviets were determined to take. The plan was to attack the salient from the north and south and, once the two arms of the pincer had met, to eliminate all the Germans remaining trapped inside. The attack went in on 25 January and the Germans were soon being overwhelmed by sheer force of numbers and the two arms of the Soviet pincer met at the village of Zvenigorodka on 28 January. Some 55,000 German troops in

six divisions were isolated in what became known as the "Cherkassy pocket" and another "Stalingrad" appeared to be on the cards.

The Soviet commanders knew something that the Germans did not: that the area was subjected to a period known locally as the rasputitsa, during which short-lived periods of warm weather unfroze the Ukrainian steppe, creating an ocean of black, viscous mud, which then froze solid again. The Soviet generals knew that the tracks of their T-34 tanks were designed for such conditions, while those of the Germans were not, and they set about making logistic preparations for what was to come; thus, when the rasputitsa started on the night of 1 February, the Soviet Army simply switched to air resupply for its forward units, while the Ilyushin shturmovik ground-attack aircraft pounded the floundering German tanks.

Two Soviet armies attacked the pocket, the fighting becoming so intense that for the German troops inside it became known as the "kessel" (cauldron) . The Soviet commanders watched as Manstein assembled a relief force to fight its way through and when it moved they formed massive ambushes in which Soviet tanks, T-34s and KV-1s, supported by shturmoviki from the air, destroyed large numbers of enemy tanks. Inside the pocket the Germans still had several airfields and, despite the snow and mud on the ground and

Soviet fighters in the air, *Luftwaffe* transports managed to fly-in over 2,000 tons of supplies, mainly fuel and ammunition.

Hitler had been determined that the troops inside the pocket should hold out but in the end he gave way to Manstein's requests, and the latter ordered the troops in the pocket to prepare to break out. Meanwhile, however, the weather was increasing its adverse effects on the Germans. The two airfields had become unusable due to mud and then it started to rain by day, turning virtually the entire pocket into a quagmire, and then refreeze at night, turning the mud into concrete.

By mid-February the Soviet armies had reduced the pocket to about 5 miles (8km) in diameter and increased the pressure, although, having halted the relief force, they realised that the Germans inside the kessel must soon attempt a breakout. This came on the clear, moonless night of 16/17 February and the Soviet forces quickly realised that the Germans were using several axes in their attempts to reach the positions where the relief force had stalled. In the darkness and confusion the Soviets failed to halt several of the German columns, but the T-34s of 5th Guards Tank Army caught a huge column in the open at 0430 and wrought terrible destruction, although the *Waffen-SS Division Wiking*

managed to reach a small forest, while a rearguard, also *Waffen-SS* troops, tried to hold the T-34s at bay using only sub-machine guns; they died to a man but managed to create a brief delay.

The Soviet T-34s harried the Germans at every turn, causing large-scale casualties, but never actually managing to stop the retreat. Many of the Germans even managed to cross a bitterly cold, deep, fast-flowing but narrow river, the Gniloy Tikich, even though when they emerged their sodden uniforms immediately froze solid.

Eventually, some 35,000 of the original 55,000 Germans in the Cherkassy pocket managed to escape, which was a triumph of sorts. On the other hand three divisions had ceased to exist, a loss the Germans could ill afford. Numbers of T-34s had been lost when attacked by German infantry and others had been lost by anti-tank fire. Overall, however, the Soviet T-34 had proved much more capable of dealing with the dreadful conditions, had consistently outgunned the German *panzers* and, although they had suffered losses, the Soviet factories were producing T-34s at a rate much greater than the Germans could destroy them. In that lay the seed of the Germans' ultimate defeat.

A12 MATILDA II

COUNTRY OF ORIGIN: Great Britain.

TYPE: infantry tank.

IN SERVICE: 1939–1945.

COMBAT WEIGHT: 59,360lb (26,926kg).

DIMENSIONS: length 18.4ft (5.6m); width 8.5ft (2.6m); height 8.3ft (2.5m).

ENGINE: two AEC six-cylinder in-line diesel engines; total 174bhp.

PERFORMANCE: road speed 15mph (24km/h); cross-country speed 8mph (13km/h); range 160 miles (256km); trench 7.0ft (2.1m).

POWER-TO-WEIGHT ratio: 7.2hp/ton.

ARMOUR: 0.5in (14mm) minimum; 3.0in (78mm) maximum.

WEAPONS: 1 x 2-pounder (40mm) main gun; 1 x 7.92in BESA coaxial MG.

AMMUNITION: 2-pounder (40mm) – 67 rounds; 7.92mm – 2,000 rounds.

CREW: four.

ABOVE: *For its day, the Matilda II had heavy armour and good firepower, but was very slow, with a maximum speed of 15mph (24km/h). However, that was as fast as the British required for an "infantry" tank.*

DESIGN HISTORY

In the inter-war years the British Army developed two types of tank: the "cruiser" tank for rapid armoured thrusts and anti-tank warfare, and the "infantry" tank for close support of infantry, particularly in the attack. Thus, the infantry tank needed to have good armoured protection, to be armed with a weapon which could deal with enemy infantry, gun positions and tanks, but did not require to be much faster than the infantry, whose average speed of advance (on foot) was reckoned to be 3mph (5km/h).

The A11 Matilda I tank entered production in 1937 and although it saw service in France in 1940, where its armoured protection proved to be adequate against German anti-tank guns, it was generally an unsatisfactory design. Work on a new infantry tank had, however, already begun, leading to the A12 Matilda II, which, despite its name, had no relationship to the Matilda I apart from the fact that both were infantry tanks.

The Matilda II had three compartments in the hull, with the driver at the front, sitting centrally behind the nose plate. Unusually among contemporary tanks there was no hull machine gun. The turret housed three men (commander, loader/operator, gunner) and was cramped, but was one of the first to be driven by hydraulic (as opposed to electric) power. The rear compartment housed the two engines, one driving each track. A total of 2,987 Matilda IIs were built.

The next version, Matilda IIA, replaced the Vickers 0.303in coaxial machine gun with the 7.92mm Besa. The Matilda IIA* had two 95hp Leyland engines in place of the AECs, while the Matilda IIA** had improved transmission and engines, and larger fuel tanks to extend the range.

NIBEIWA AND TUMMAR WEST: 9 DECEMBER 1940

The Italian African Army, some 250,000 strong and commanded by Marshal Graziani attacked the British in the Western Desert in September 1940; the British force, heavily outnumbered, fell back in good order before them. Despite his numerical superiority, Graziani halted after penetrating only a short distance into Egyptian territory and established his army in a series of fortified encampments. The British General Wavell decided that such a supine enemy deserved to be attacked and issued the necessary orders to General O'Connor, commanding Western Desert Force (one armoured and one infantry division [32,000 men]).

The British attack was launched at first light on 9 December 1940, one element being 11th Indian Brigade, which consisted of three infantry battalions (2nd Cameron Highlanders, 1/6th Rajputana Rifles, 4/7th Rajput Regiment), with support for this operation from an armoured regiment, 7th Battalion Royal Tank Regiment (7RTR), equipped with Matilda IIs. 11th Brigade's first objective was the armed camp at Nibeiwa, held by an Italian divisional size force, designated Gruppo Maletti after its commander. 4/7th Rajputs carried out diversionary attacks on the north-east corner of the camp in the middle of the night, covering the noise of 7 RTR's tanks moving around the camp to the south. So, when 7 RTR attacked at first light they achieved complete surprise and were able to destroy all 23 Italian M11 tanks within 10 minutes. The Italian defence was very courageous, General Maletti, carrying only a pistol, being killed attacking a Matilda II, and artillerymen firing at the advancing Matilda IIs, over open sights until they were killed. The Matilda IIs performance was outstanding; their armour was so thick that Italian shells bounced off, while the British 2-pounder (46mm) ammunition passed straight through the thin armour of the Italian tanks. The camp eventually fell at about 1000 after a fierce battle in which the Italians lost several hundred dead and 4,000 captured, while 7RTR lost two dead and six wounded.

After only a brief pause, 11th Brigade moved on to attack the next camp, Tummar West, from the west across the open desert. That fell after less than an hour, following which the British troops reorganised and rested in preparation for further attacks the next day. British tanks and their guns gained a bad reputation in the years 1939–1942, but, as this day's battles showed, the Matilda II was impervious to anything the Italian Army could use against them, while the much-maligned 2-pounder (46mm) gun was highly effective against Italian tanks.

BELOW: *The Matilda II was armed with a 2-pounder gun whose performance was better than that of the 37mm in the German army's PzKpfw III.*

ABOVE: *The Matilda II, as used by 7RTR during its attack on the Italian fortified camps at Nibeiwa and Tummar West; the Italians had nothing to match it.*

RIGHT: *The Baron anti-mine tank was created by removing the turret from a Matilda II and adding the flail with two 75hp engines to drive it.*

A22 CHURCHILL MARK III

DESIGN HISTORY

In July 1940 Vauxhall Motors, was instructed to design, test and start production of a new infantry tank within 12 months. The company had the first prototype running within seven months and the first 14 production Churchill Is left the line in June 1941. Such rapid development left some problems, which took time to resolve; for example, the "twin-six" engine consisted of two horizontally opposed Bedford truck engines united by a common crankcase, giving a compact and powerful engine, but which was also complex and difficult to maintain.

The Churchill I was armed with a 2-pounder (40mm) gun and a 3in close support howitzer, mounted in the vertical bow-plate, with the gunner sitting alongside the driver. From the Churchill II onwards, however, this howitzer was replaced by a 0.30in Besa machine gun, while in the Churchill III the main armament was the much more effective 6-pounder (57mm). Protection was good and the interior spacious, and the Churchill was the first British tank to use the Merritt-Brown regenerative steering system. The suspension system used 11, independently sprung bogies on each side, which gave a harsh ride but was both simple and cheap, and absorbed a lot of damage before affecting the tank's mobility.

BELOW: *Churchill I with a turret-mounted 2-pdr (40mm) gun and a close support 3in (76mm) howitzer in the hull, beside the driver. Only a few were built.*

BELOW: *A few Churchill IIIs saw action at the Battle of El Alamein in the Western Desert and similar Mark IIIs took part in the Battle of Steamroller Farm in Tunisia.*

STEAMROLLER FARM: 28 FEBRUARY 1943

Six Churchills took part in the Dieppe raid (19 August 1942) and all were captured, placing the type's future in considerable doubt; indeed, some thought was given to ending production, but all this was changed by its performance in Tunisia. The Allies were advancing when the Germans launched a series of attacks on 25/26 February 1943 against the northern part of the Allied line ,in the course of which the British No. 6 Commando was surrounded at Steamroller Farm, just north of the small town of El Aroussa, by six companies of German paratroops, supported by seven PzKpfw III/IV tanks, four armoured cars and an anti-tank unit armed with 88mm guns; the Germans took the position, with most of the British commandoes escaping. On 27 February, A Squadron 51 Royal Tank Regiment (A Sqn, 51 RTR) was ordered to conduct a strong probe towards the German positions, with support from infantry, artillery and engineers.

A Sqn's dozen Churchill Mk IIIs approached Steamroller Farm with two troops forward and the infantry riding on the tanks of the second wave. At about 1600 they came under heavy fire and after an initial redeployment they reorganised to carry out an attack. But at that moment they were themselves attacked by Ju-87s which, in combination with the 88mm guns, quickly knocked out a number of tanks, leaving just nine runners. A Sqn commander reported the situation to his superior, only to be

told to "push on at all costs," so he ordered Lieutenant Hollands, commanding No.1 Troop to advance. Hollands actually had only one tank left, but, obedient to the last order, he advanced and soon found himself facing an 88m gun at 50yd (00m) range. The Churchill was temporarily unable to fire owing to a 6-pounder (40mm) ammunition problem while the machine gunner was reloading his BESA, so the "88" was able to fire twice, but the first round hit a storage bin and the second missed altogether.

At this point the machine gunner brought his BESA into action, forcing the enemy to abandon their "88", and then mowed them down as they fled. A second "88" was then destroyed, following which two PzKpfw IIIs appeared and were also hit, forcing their crews to abandon them. By this time a second Churchill had arrived and the two tanks proceeded to destroy the German supply trucks which were lined up near the farm.

The two Churchills then withdrew to the main British position but the German paratroops were so shattered by the experience that they withdrew in the night and the British were then able to continue their advance. This action resulted in Captain Hollands receiving the immediate award of the Distinguished Service Order, but it also resulted in the restoration of the reputation of the Churchill tank.

ABOVE: *Although slow, the Churchill had excellent cross-country ability and was particularly effective in mountainous terrain, such as that found in Tunisia and Italy. The forward extensions carrying the tracks, known to the crews as "horns", greatly reduced the driver's vision and the field-of-fire of the bow machinegunner.*

RIGHT: *Churchill III with turret-mounted 6-pdr (57mm) gun and hull-mounted 7.92mm MG in place of the 3in howitzer. Normal range was a derisory 90 miles (144km) and the jettisonable external fuel tank gave much-needed extra range. This was the model used by 7 RTR at Steamroller Farm in February 1943.*

A34 Comet

Specifications

Country of origin: Great Britain.
Type: cruiser tank.
In service: 1944–1945.
Combat weight: 78,800lb (35,696kg).
Dimensions: length 21.5 (6.6m); width 10.0ft (3.1m); height 8.8ft (2.8m).
Engine: Rolls-Royce Meteor Mark 3 V-12 water-cooled, petrol engine; 600bhp at 2,550rpm.
Performance: road speed 32mph (51km/h); range 123 miles (196km); trench 8.0ft (2.4m); gradient 35 per cent.
Power-to-weight ratio: 17hp/ton.
Ground pressure: 13.85lb/sq in (0.88kg/sq cm).
Armour: 0.6in (14mm) minimum; 4.0in (102mm) maximum.
Weapons: 1 x QF 77mm main gun; 1 x 7.92in BESA coaxial MG; 1 x 7.92mm BESA hull-mounted MG.
Ammunition: 77mm – 61 rounds; 7.92mm – 5,175 rounds.
Crew: five.

Design history

The story of British tank development during World War II is not particularly edifying, but it ended on a reasonable note with the A34 Comet which just managed to reach service before the end of hostilities in Europe. The Challenger tank, which started development in 1942 and reached service in 1944, was not a great success, mainly because it was created by mounting the new and powerful 17-pounder gun on a Cromwell hull which was too small for the stresses involved. Thus, a new tank was required, the first step being to select the gun, which boiled down to a choice between the American 76mm and a new British High Velocity

RIGHT AND BELOW: *For most people the Comet was the tank all British developments had been leading up to, being fast, agile, well-armed and with a good range. This is the tank of the Commanding Officer, 1st Royal Tank Regiment (1RTR) in Berlin in summer 1945. Note the red "Desert Rat" insignia of the famed 7th Armoured Division.*

(HV) gun of the same calibre but firing different ammunition. To avoid confusion, especially on the battlefield, the new British gun was called the "77mm".

Leyland Motors started design work on the new tank in February 1943 and presented a proposal to the General Staff in July and a mock-up in September. The hull design was based on that of the Cromwell, but with extra armour, and the Christie suspension was also similar, with five road wheels each side, but with stronger springing to cope with the extra weight and the addition of five return rollers. Cross-country performance was especially good, the Comet proving both fast and agile; a limiting factor was crew discomfort.

The new gun, however, required a larger turret and the turret ring was increased from 57in (145cm) in the Cromwell to 64in (163cm) in the Comet, but this was achieved without the necessity for widening the hull. In October 1943 a production order was placed, with 20 pre-production tanks to be ready by June 1944.

The hull was all-welded with a well-sloped bow plate, but with a vertical section necessary for the

ADVANCE TO THE BALTIC: MARCH–APRIL 1945

The first formation to convert to the Comet was 11th Armoured Division which started the process in Belgium in December 1944, although this was disrupted briefly by the German Ardennes offensive. Having carried out thorough training, the division moved up to the Wesel bridgehead on the eastern bank of the Rhine on 11 March 1945, from where it advanced over a five-week period until it reached Lübeck on the Baltic coast.

The verdict on the Comet was that it was a splendid tank, and that the 77mm gun was the most accurate tank gun anyone had ever handled, athough its projectiles would not always penetrate the front plates of the German Panther. The gun also fired very effective high-explosive (HE) shells, which were used regularly against snall "stay-behind" parties which had been specifically tasked by the retreating Germans to conduct tank ambushes.

During this brief period, the Comet proved to be thoroughly reliable and very fast on both roads and cross-country, which could not have been said of many British World War II tanks. In fact, the troops had handled the Comet considered it to be a real battle-winner, their only criticism being that it had taken the British Army so long to get such a good tank into service.

bow machine gun. The driver sat on the right and the bow gunner on the left. The turret was also all-welded with a suspended basket, with the commander and gunner on the left of the main gun and the loader on the right. The 77mm gun was a modified version of the 17-pounder (76.2mm) gun, with a shorter barrel and a redesigned chamber. It had a good anti-tank and HE performance, and also proved to be exceptionally accurate. The ammunition was stowed in armoured bins to give better protection against splinters and fire, and was a very welcome development for the crews.

The Comet was not without its critics (but no tank ever is!). Some combat veterans criticised the retention of the hull machine gun and gunner, which had not proved of any value in service. They also did not like the vertical section of the bow-plate, which was required to mount the machine gun, but which was very vulnerable to the latest anti-tank projectiles. Similarly, they thought the belly armour too weak for modern anti-tank mines. Time was not available to remedy these faults, although it seems odd with hindsight that all three had not been thought of earlier.

ABOVE: *The Comet was armed with the very accurate and effective British 77mm high-velocity gun, for which it carried 61 rounds*

LEFT: *A Comet on the move during the closing stages of the war; it saw action but mostly against scattered pockets of resistance.*

M3 LIGHT TANK

DESIGN HISTORY

The standard US light tank in the late 1930s was the M2A4, which was constructed from rivetted armour plate, weighed 12 tons (12,193kg), and was armed with a 37mm gun. This was improved, uparmoured and given a stronger suspension system. The resulting vehicle was considered sufficiently different to be given a new designation as the M3A1.

The M3A1 was slightly heavier than the M2A4 at 12.2 tons (12,400kg), but retained the 37mm gun, which was fitted with a gyro-stabiliser enabling it to be fired on the move; the turret was fabricated from welded homogenous steel and also had power traverse. Secondary armament consisted of no fewer than four 0.30in machine guns, one of which was mounted coaxially with the main gun while the second was in a flexible mounting on the turret roof to provide anti-aircraft defence. The other two were more unconventional, being mounted in fixed, forward-firing mountings, one on each side of the hull, although they proved to be of limited value and were often dis-mounted and the space used for equipment storage.

Power was provided by a seven-cylinder Continental radial engine, which had been developed for land use from an aircraft engine, but when supplies ran low in 1941 500 M3s were fitted with the Guiberson T-1020 diesel engine. Battle experience with the British Army showed that the range was too low, as a result of which two jettisonable external tanks were developed.

Combat experience in the Pacific of dealing with one bunker after another, all manned by Japanese soldiers determined to fight to the death, led to the development of two types of M3 flame-thrower tank. One, known as "Satan", had the flamethrower in place of the 37mm gun, while in the other the flamethrower replaced the hull machine gun. These M3 flame-throwers were used at Saipan, Tinian and Guam, but thereafter were replaced by flamethrower versions of the M4 Sherman.

The M3 was by far the most widely used light tank in World War II and when production ended in October 1943 some 13,859 had been produced.

ABOVE LEFT: *US Marine Corps M3A1 on Guadalcanal in September 1942. Main gun is 37mm and there are four machine guns: one coaxial, two in hull sponsons and one on the turret roof.*

LEFT: *A late model M3; note that there is no machine gun in the hull sponson and that the aperture has been capped. Although it had short-comings, it was reliable. and popular with its users.*

LEFT AND BELOW: *The most widely used light tank in World War II,* some 14,000 MR3s had been produced by April 1945.

BETIO ISLAND: NOVEMBER 1943

The M3 fought in numerous campaigns in the early years of World War II and was so popular with British Army cavalry units using it as a reconnaissance vehicle in the North African campaign that they nicknamed it the "Honey." The M3 was also very well-regarded by the US Marine Corps and was the mainstay of their armoured units in the early battles on the Pacific islands, as the tide of Japanese expansion was gradually turned back. A Marine Light Tank Battalion consisted of 72 M3s.

The M3 was light, agile and mechanically reliable, which made it ideal for the terrible "going" on the Pacific islands, and enabled it to go to places where the heavier Sherman could not. On the other hand, its armoured protection was poor and its 37mm gun was ineffective against the strongest Japanese pillboxes. Nevertheless, it was considered a vital element of an invasion force.

The Tarawa atoll is composed of some 24 coral islets, one of which is Betio, which has an area of only some 300 acres (121 hectares), but during the Pacific island-hopping campaign was the site of an airfield and was defended by some 3,000 determined Japanese naval infantry. The assault landing by 2d Marine Division took place on 20 November 1943 and the first hazard was that there was an unexpectedly low tide, which meant that M3 commanders had to wade through the shallows between the coral reef and the beach, moving ahead of their tanks to choose the route to the shore – all under fire. Then, once on the beach they were faced by a 4ft (1.2m) sea-wall made of palm logs, which was covered by machine gun and artillery fire and caused the M3s severe problems. These were eventually overcome and the M3s then hurried inland to give much-needed support of the Marines infantry.

On several occasions the M3s provided essential support. Two of them, operating in conjunction with 5in (127mm) gunfire from destroyers in the lagoon, enabled 3d Battalion, 2d Marines to clear the western end of the island, thus opening the way for reinforcements to land. The M3 may have been small, light and inadequately armed, but in the Pacific landings in 1942 and 1943 it provided crucial help to the Marines.

M3 Grant/Lee

DESIGN HISTORY

This unusual design resulted from analysis of the early operations in Europe in 1939 which made it clear that the US Army's existing 37mm tank gun was insufficiently powerful for modern warfare. It was therefore, decided to produce a new tank, with a large, box-like hull, topped by a turret-mounted 37mm gun, but which also had a large sponson mounting a 75mm gun. This new vehicle, the M3, was ordered straight from the drawing-board in July 1940, but was primarily intended as an interim design pending the arrival of the M4 Sherman. Pilot models of the M3 were running in April 1941; production started in August 1941 and ended in December 1942, by which time 6,258 had been built.

Various models were built, some with cast hulls and others with welded hulls, and a variety of powerplants were installed. The intended powerplant of the M3 was the Wright Cyclone radial

SPECIFICATIONS

COUNTRY OF ORIGIN: United States of America.
TYPE: medium tank.
IN SERVICE: 1941–1944.
COMBAT WEIGHT: 60,000lb (27,216kg).
DIMENSIONS: length 18.5ft (5.6m); width 8.9ft (2.7m); height 10.3ft (3.1m).
ENGINE: Wright Continental R-975-EC2 nine-cylinder air-cooled radial petrol engine; 340hp at 2,400rpm (see below).
PERFORMANCE: road speed 26mph (42km/h); cross-country speed 16mph (26km/h); range 120 miles (193km); trench 6.3ft (1.9m); gradient 60 per cent.
GROUND PRESSURE: 13.4lb/sq in (0.9kg/sq cm).
POWER-TO-WEIGHT ratio: 12.7hp/ton.
ARMOUR: 0.5in (12mm) minimum; 1.5in (37mm) maximum.
WEAPONS: 1 x 75mm M2/M3 gun in hull sponson; 1 x 37mm M5/M6 gun in turret; 1 x 0.30in M1919A4 coaxial MG; 2 x 0.30in M1919A4 MG in bow (fixed mounting); 1 x 0.30in MG in cupola on turret roof (British Grant only).
AMMUNITION: 75mm – 41 rounds.

LEFT: *M3 tanks in service with the US Army. The figure standing beside the leading tank gives a good idea of the considerable height of these vehicles – 10.3ft (3.1m) to the top of the cupola .*

RIGHT: *This frontal view of the M3 shows the very large area presented to an enemy anti-tank gun, but the sponson mounting was the only way of getting a 75mm gun into service quickly. The M3 required a large crew: commander, driver and two men (gunner and loader) on each gun.*

and many had this engine, but when demand exceeded supply various alternatives were introduced. One such engine used two GM 6-71 diesels coupled together, another had five ordinary automobile engines coupled together (nicknamed "The Eggbeater"), while Guiberson diesels were also installed in some models.

There was a crew of six: commander, driver, gunner and loader for 37mm gun, and gunner and loader for 75mm gun. This caused some overcrowding problems, making life especially uncomfortable in the hot African climate.

The majority of M3s went to the US Army, but a significant number were supplied to the British under Lend-Lease, all of them going to the 8th Army in the Western Desert, apart from a few for training, which went to the UK. The British took delivery of all the various types of M3 as used by the US Army, which were known as the General Lee in British service. There was also a version with the standard US Army hull and 75mm gun, but with a British-designed turret, which could be recognised by the commander's cupola atop the turret; this was known as the General Grant.

BATTLE OF ALAMEIN: OCTOBER/NOVEMBER 1942

Grant Is started to arrive in the Western Desert in early 1942 and were at the Battle of Gazala (27 May 1942). They were followed by some 350 more, which played a significant role in the Battle of Alamein (23 October – 4 November 1942). In this battle the British Lieutenant-General Montgomery had deployed XXX Corps in the north and XIII Corps in the south, but with the bulk of his tanks were concentrated in X Corps behind XXX Corps; a total of some 195,000 men and 1,000 tanks. Montgomery's opponent was Field Marshal Rommel, commanding a mixed German and Italian army of some 104,000 men and 500 tanks.

The battle opened with a dense artillery barrage at 2140 23 October, with a strong attack in the north and a diversionary attack in the south, the latter being sufficiently strong to prevent the Axis moving their armour reserves to the north. Rommel was in Germany on sick leave when the battle started and returned late on 25 October, but even his touch failed to prevent the continuing British success. Montgomery launched Operation Supercharge at 0100 on 2 November, which succeeded, despite several counterattacks and major losses in tanks. The British could afford such losses, however, but the Axis could not and by 3 November, by when he had just 35 tanks left, Rommel started a fighting withdrawal, which was to continue, with a few brief halts, until the last remnants were

evacuated from Tunisia some months later.

Inevitably, the M3 suffered some disadvantages. It was very bulky and over 10ft (3m) high, while the sponson-mounting of the 75mm gun meant that it could not adopt a hull-down firing position. Nevertheless, it was a good tank for its time, could defeat the PzKpfw IV/75 and was well thought of in the British 8th Army.

TOP RIGHT: *The crew of a US-supplied British 8th Army General Grant tank inspect the damage they have just inflicted on a German PzKpfw I light tank. Such a lightly armoured vehicle would have stood no chance against the Grant's powerful 75mm gun. Note also the additional stowage bins on the British tank's front trackguards and the rear engine decking.*

CENTRE RIGHT: *British General Lee, with sponson-mounted 75mm, and turret-mounted 37mm gun with commander's cupola, horizontal volute suspension, side door, and rivetted hull.*

RIGHT: *US Army M3 in swamp country. Although produced in large numbers, the M3 was an "interim" design awaiting the arrival of the M4 Sherman.*

M4 Sherman

Specifications

Country of origin: United States of America.
Type: medium tank.
In service: 1942–1945.
Combat weight: 69,565lb (31,544kg).
Dimensions: length 20.6ft (6.3m); width 8.9ft (2.7m); height 11.0ft (3.4m).
Engine: Ford GAA V-8 water-cooled in-line petrol engine; 500hp at 2,600rpm (see below).
Performance: road speed 26mph (42km/h); range 100 miles (160km); trench 7.5ft (2.3m); gradient 60 per cent.
Ground pressure: 14.3lb/sq in (1.0kg/sq cm).
Power-to-weight ratio: 16.9hp/ton.
Armour: 0.6in (15mm) minimum; 3.9in (100mm) maximum.
Weapons: 1 x 75mm M3 gun in turret; 1 x 0.30in M1919A4 coaxial MG; 1 x 0.30in M1919A4 MG in ball-mount in bow-plate; 1 x 0.50in M2 MG in flexible mount on turret roof; one 2in smoke mortar in turret roof.
Crew: five.

Design history

On 29 August 1940, the day following the decision to produce the M3 Grant/Lee, work began on a new tank with the 75mm gun mounted in a fully revolving turret rather than a sponson. The new design used many components of the M3, including the lower hull, suspension, engine and drive-train, and was standardised in September 1941 as the M4 General Sherman.

The turret was a one-piece casting 3in (76.2mm) thick at the front, and power-operated, while the gun was gyrostabilised in elevation. The lower hull was welded and standard across the different models, but there were two types of upper hull, the first being welded and angular (M4), while the other was cast and rounded (M4A1). Other variations

Below: *This Sherman has had the bow machine gun replaced by a flame-thrower, a fearsome weapon which was used against enemy in bunkers. It had a range of some 40yd (37m), but did not detract from the use of the tank's normal gun, which in this case is the original short-barrelled 75mm M3.*

were mainly due to the type of engine, gun and suspension.

Like the M3 Grant/Lee, the M4 Sherman production programme was affected by supply shortages of the Wright radial engine, and a variety of alternatives were fitted. These included a 450hp Ford, the Chrysler five-bank radial arrangement of six-cylinder, in-line engines, and the General Motors twin diesel, the latter being favoured by the crews, since it was more reliable and less of a fire risk.

The first Shermans mounted the 75mm (2.95in) M2 gun, which had a short (31 calibre) barrel , resulting in low muzzle velocity of 1,850ft/sec (564m/s). This was replaced by the M3 75mm (2.95in) gun with a longer (40 calibre) barrel, firing armour-piercing shot at a muzzle velocity of 2,030ft/sec (619m/s); it also had a much improved breech. Even this gun was rapidly outdated by improvements in German firepower and protection, leading to a new 3in (76.2mm) tank gun (generally known as the "76mm") with a muzzle velocity firing

high velocity armour piercing (HVAP) projectiles of 3,400ft/sec (1,040m/s). This 55 calibre gun was noticeably longer than earlier weapons and had a muzzle brake, while the new T23 turret was more angular than earlier turrets and was fitted with a bustle to act as a counterweight. These were installed from late 1943 onwards.

Early Shermans had a tendency to "brew-up" (catch fire) when hit by anti-tank projectiles, so much so that for a while British soldiers referred to them, ironically, as "Ronsons", after a well-known make of cigarette lighter. Various efforts were made to overcome this, mainly by protecting the ammunition stowed in the tank, moving them to the bottom of the hull and surrounding them by water jackets.

To facilitate rapid production, early Shermans were fitted with the same "vertical volute" suspension and 14in (410mm) wide track as those on the earlier M2 medium tank, but these took little account of the increase in weight from 20 to over 30

LEFT: *M4 Shermans with the British 8th Army in the North African desert in November 1942. The Sherman introduced new standards of reliability and effectiveness.*

BELOW: *US Army M4 Sherman armed with the 76mm main gun, which can be distinguished by its long barrel and muzzle brake. This 55-calibre weapon was far more effective than the earlier 75mm and entered service in late 1943.*

LEFT AND ABOVE LEFT: *The M4A3E8 seen here can be identified as Tank No. 12 of A Company, 191st Tank Battalion, of 7th (US) Army. It is armed with a long-barrelled 76mm gun and is fitted with the HVSS suspension which led its crews to name this model the "East Eight" because of its excellent ride. The 0.50in M2 machine gun, normally mounted on a pintle on the turret roof is stored in this case at the rear of the turret.*

RIGHT: *Shermans in the Ardennes, winter 1944/45.*

BELOW RIGHT: *A mixed force in action, including Shermans (foreground, top right), Churchill flame-throwers and carriers.*

BELOW: *Sherman and infantry of the US Army's 11th Armored Division advance through a burning village, Germany, April.*

OPERATION GOODWOOD: 18 – 21 JULY 1944

Operation Goodwood emphasised both the strengths and weaknesses of the Sherman. The British and Canadians landed on the Allied left on D-day (6 June 1944), with United States forces on the right. Both then sought to expand their beach-heads against desperate and increasingly strong German resistance. US forces captured Cherbourg (27 June) giving the Allies a port and consolidating their rear, while at the front the Americans were opposed by the German Seventh Army (seven divisions) while Panzer Group West (seven armoured, two infantry divisions) faced the British/Canadians. But by 10 July there was intelligence that Panzer Lehr division had arrived on the American front and that German infantry was relieving armoured units on the British/Canadian front, enabling the latter to move to confront the Americans as well. British Lieutenant-General Montgomery therefore ordered the British/Canadian forces to initiate armoured operations east of the River Orne between Caen and Falaise (Operation Goodwood). This was intended to increase the threat to the Germans, forcing them to deploy yet more panzer units to face the British, thus enabling

the Americans to break out and to continue their advance to Avranches.

The Germans expected an attack, but the opening stroke took them by surprise, when the Allies unleashed a four-hour, pre-attack bombardment in which 7,000 tons of ordnance were delivered to a 10-mile square area east and south-east of Caen. It began at 0530 on 18 July with 1,000 RAF heavy bombers dropping 2,500 tons of bombs in 45 minutes, followed by shelling from a combination of Royal Navy ships and army artillery, and finally by attack by 600 USAAF heavy bombers. On the ground H-hour was 0745 and the first attack by 11th Armoured Division started well as stunned German survivors tried to recover, while the major British problem seemed to be some traffic congestion at the bridges.

Then, contrary to all expectations, the Germans began to recover, with the British experiencing their first major setback at Cagny, where defending 88mm guns knocked out 12 Shermans within a minute. There were also eight Tiger Is in the village and a tremendous battle was soon raging, in which many British tanks, mostly Shermans, were lost in the open country around the village.

tons. After considerable trials, a new "horizontal volute" suspension system (HVSS) and a 23in (580mm) track was adopted, which considerably improved the cross-country ride. This version's official US Army designation was M4A3E8, leading to its US nickname of "Easy 8".

Numerous versions were produced, including self-propelled guns and rocket-launchers, but only two are of interest here. The Sherman DD (= duplex drive) was an ordinary gun tank fitted with a screen and twin propellers, making it fully amphibious; it could swim rivers or be launched offshore and, on arrival at the far bank or the beach, drop the skirt and go straight into action. The British "Sherman Firefly VC" mounted the British 17-pounder (76.2mm) gun; it was a very effective tank-killer; one of them being responsible for killing SS-Major Wittmann in Normandy.

Critics concentrated on the Sherman's deficiencies and it is true that in a one-on-one confrontation the odds would be on a Panther. However, the Sherman more than made up for its shortcomings by much superior reliability, easier field maintenance, greater endurance, and its vast numbers, with which, in the end, it overwhelmed the German panzers. By the time the production lines closed 49,230 had been produced and the Sherman was the standard medium tank of the US Army and Marine Corps, and the Free French Army, while large numbers also served in the British and Soviet armies, although both the latter also used large numbers of their own tank designs.

TOP RIGHT: *British Army amphibious Sherman DD (duplex drive); note lowered flotation screen and twin propellers at rear.*

RIGHT: *Canadian Army Shermans' Normandy, 1944. The track sections and sand-bags increased protection against anti-tank projectiles.*

This lasted all day, with the higher commands on both sides unable to impose any control on this tank-versus-tank slogging match. But, despite heavy losses, by 1800 the British had established a foothold on the edge of the village.

Elsewhere, two British armoured regiments attacked the villages of Bras and Hubert Folie and, as at Cagny, both were caught in the open by "88s" and SP guns, quickly joined by Panthers, and by noon there were many burning tanks on the battlefield. On the right flank of the British attack Canadians fought their way into the steelworks at Colombelles and by the end of the first day casualties in men were heavy. However, the British/Canadians had lost 200 tanks against the Germans' 109.

On 19 July the British/Canadians resumed their advance but again made slow progress. In the afternoon 11th Armoured Division attacked Bras and literally wiped out the defending infantry battalion, but at heavy cost: 3rd Royal Tank Regiment, for example, lost 54 of its 63 tanks in the first 48 hours. Another battle raged all day for the village of Bourgébus, where Tiger Is and "88s" resisted all attempts by 7th Armoured Division to take it.

By this time both sides were reaching the limits of endurance, but the following day (20 June) 7th Armoured Division renewed its attack on Bourgébus only to discover that the enemy had withdrawn. The battle moved south to the Verrières ridge south of Caen, which was being held by about 100 tanks, mostly Tiger Is and Panthers. Then, however, a violent rainstorm, lasting 48 hours, caused extensive flooding, turning most of the area into a sea of mud. Operation Goodwood then petered out, with the troops on both sides exhausted and Allied commanders frustrated by what appeared to be a failure to achieve the aim.

The operation was an undoubted strategic success, the Germans having brought many reserves on to the British front, as Montgomery had planned. The British/Canadian forces had started the battle with 750 tanks and lost 413 of them, while the Germans started with 230 and lost approximately 100, but the difference was that the Germans could ill afford such losses, while the Shermans would continue to roll off the production lines in the United States at a far higher rate than the Germans could ever destroy them.

LANDING VEHICLE, TRACKED MARK 4 (LVT4)

DESIGN HISTORY

There had long been a US Marine Corps requirement for an amphibious vehicle which could transfer loads from ships to shore and, if necessary, move some distance inland. One solution originated in 1935, when Donald Reeling unveiled an amphibious vehicle known as the Alligator, which was intended for use in the Florida Everglades on civilian flood-relief and rescue missions. This vehicle had a large-volume, lightweight hull fabricated from duralumin and was fitted with special tracks with bolt-on "grosser" to increase their thrust in water, thus using the tracks

SPECIFICATIONS
COUNTRY OF ORIGIN: United States of America.
TYPE: amphibious, tracked fighting/logistics vehicle.
IN SERVICE: 1942–1945.
COMBAT WEIGHT: unloaded, 23,350lb (10,600kg).
DIMENSIONS: length 26.1ft (8.0m); width 10.6ft (3.2m); height 8.2ft (2.5m).
ENGINE: Continental seven-cylinder, radial, aircooled, petrol engine; 200hp at 1,800rpm.
PERFORMANCE: waterborne 5.4kt; road speed 25mph (40km/h); water range 75 miles (121km), road range 150 miles (242km).
GROUND PRESSURE: 8.4lb/sq in (0.6kg/sq cm).
POWER-TO-WEIGHT ratio: 15.4hp/ton.
ARMOUR: plastic armour sheets added as required.
WEAPONS: 1 or 2 x 0.30in M1919A4 MG; or 1 or 2 x 0.50in M2 MG (mounted if required).
CARRYING CAPACITY: men – 24 (fully equipped); or one Jeep; or one anti-tank gun; or general stores – 6,500lb (2,950kg).
CREW: three.

for propulsion on both land and water. This vehicle was followed by an improved version in 1940, incorporating lessons learnt from the 1935 model. A magazine article on this attracted the attention of the US Marine Corps, which placed an order for a vehicle made of steel rather than duralumin and with a more powerful engine. As with the civilian version, however, this vehicle, which was designated the Landing Vehicle, Tracked Mark 1 (LVT1) was unarmoured, had a rear-mounted engine and a rigid suspension. Some 1,225 of this model were built.

Next to appear was the LVT2, which incorporated a number of improvements. These mainly affected the propulsion and included a more powerful engine, "torsilastic" suspension for better cross-country performance, and cast-aluminium "grosser" for more efficient water-borne propulsion. A modified version, LVT(A)2, had increased armour and was intended for use without defensive weapons. A total of 3,413 LVT2 and LVT(A)2 were produced.

All versions up to this point had a rear-mounted engine which meant that loading and unloading had to be done over the side. The LVT 3, however,

LEFT: *LVT(A)1 was an LVT2 with a turret-mounted 37mm M6 gun. There were also a coaxial 0.30in machine gun and two more machine guns on open ring mounts behind the turret, one each side of the rear deck.*

ABOVE LEFT: *The LVT3 and LVT4 had a forward mounted engine, enabling a large cargo hold to be created. This was 12.3ft (3.7m) long and 7.0ft (2.1m) wide and with its full width stern ramp made it possible to load and unload light vehicles, such as Jeeps.*

overcame this problem with a rear-mounted ramp, enabling light vehicles such as Jeeps to be carried and which also made loading/unloading on land much easier. This displaced the rear-mounted engine and two Cadillac V-8 water-cooled engines were mounted one in each side of the vehicle with long propulsion shafts to the forward-mounted differential.

The final wartime version was the LVT(4) which retained the rear ramp of the LVT3 but had a single engine, which was mounted forward. Some 8,438 LVT4s were built.

There were also a number of "armoured" versions. The LVT(A)1 was based on the LVT2, but had a totally enclosed fighting compartment on top of which was mounted a enclosed turret, fitted with a 37mm M6 gun with a coaxial 0.30in machine gun. Two more 0.30in MGs were mounted on ring mounts behind the turret, one on either side of the vehicle. The LVT(A)2 was an up-armoured version of the LVT2 but with no extra weapons. The LVT(A)4, however, was a modified version of the LVT(A)2 but with an M8 75mm howitzer mounted in an open-topped turret.

These vehicles were given a variety of semi-official names. The LVT1 was known as the "Alligator" while the LVT2 was dubbed the "Water

PACIFIC CAMPAIGN: 1942–1945

The LVT's role was highly specialised and of relatively brief duration, providing the essential function of crossing the "water gap", that stretch of sea between the larger ships and the beach. Without the LVT, that gap would have been considerably more difficult to cross, while their advantage over landing-craft was that they could climb out of the water and move inland, a capability which was the greatest benefit to the troops in the first few hours of landing, when they were particularly vulnerable.

Following their first use in the landings on Tarawa on 11 November 1943, LVT's were used in almost all the Pacific landings. They were aso used in Europe, particularly by the British who referred to them as the "Buffalo amphibian". Large numbers were employed during the Scheldt estuary operations in October 1944, while no fewer than 600 were used by Field Marshal Montgomery's 21st Army Group in the crossing of the Rhine in March 1945. The use of the LVT was confined to a very specific role in amphibious operations, but in that it was supreme.

Buffalo" and the LVT3 the "Bushmaster". The most widely used name, however, was "Amtrac" a shortened form of the designation "Amphibious Tractor" which had been applied to a number of LVT1s supplied to the US Army.

BELOW: *LVT(A)2 climbs on to a beach on an exercise. The basic design was developed from a civilian vehicle intended for rescue missions in the Florida Everglades. It used its tracks to propel it through water at a speed* of 5.4 knots or on land at 25mph (40km/h).

RIGHT: *LVT(A)4 mounted a short-barrelled M8 75mm howitzer in an open-topped turret, further increasing amphibious firepower.*

BATTLE-WINNING AIRCRAFT

One consequence of their experiences in World War I was a general reluctance in most countries to spend money on defence projects, which resulted in development in most weapons fields being relatively slow. Aeronautics was a notable exception, however, not least because, unlike with warships and tanks, there were many developments in the closely related civilian air transportation, and there was considerable cross-fertilisation between the two. Thus, by the mid-1930s the biplane era was virtually at an end and the new military monoplanes incorporated developments such as all-metal construction, engines of ever greater power, retractable undercarriages, slats, flaps, covered cockpits and increasingly sophisticated control and instrument systems. In addition to these technological advances, much thought was given to the strategic and tactical use of air power, and useful testing grounds for both aircraft and theories on their employment were found in the numerous campaigns in the 1930s, including those undertaken by the Italians in Abyssinia, the Japanese in China, and the Germans in the Spanish Civil War.

GERMANY

As a result of the 1919 Versailles Treaty, Germany was unable to undertake overt military aircraft development until the mid-1930s, but it then established the *Luftwaffe* which rapidly became one of the most effective air arms in the world. By the outbreak of war in 1939 Germany had one of the best all-round fighters in service, the Messerschmitt Bf 109; a widely feared dive-bomber, the Junkers Ju 87 Stuka; and a bomber force which operated with ruthless efficiency in the Polish and French campaigns. The *Luftwaffe* then went on to meet its first serious set-back in the Battle of Britain and, despite early successes in the Balkans and on the Eastern Front, it was increasingly put on the defensive by the Allied air forces. Radical developments such as the jet-propelled Messerschmitt Me 262 fighter and Arado Ar 234 bomber, and the Messerschmitt Me 162 rocket-powered interceptor appeared too late and in too small numbers to affect the issue.

Somewhat surprisingly, German development of strategic bombers was very limited. The twin-engined types, such as the Heinkel He 111 and Junkers Ju 88, were not particular effective and the *Luftwaffe* never possessed an adequate four-engined bomber to compare with the British Lancaster and Halifax or the United States' B-17 and B-24. In the end, the *Luftwaffe*, despite the courage of its aircrews, proved unable either to support the army in the field or, even more tellingly, to protect Germany's civil population from the incessant bombing raids.

ITALY

Despite all the bombast from Mussolini the Italians never produced any military aircraft of any significance. The country entered the war in 1940 with a number of under-powered and inadequately armed fighters and bombers, and it was only when manufacturers decided to import the German Daimler-Benz DB-601 engines and MG 151 cannon that any improvements were made. Prototypes of some new types were flown and a few production machines appeared, but in 1943 Italy signed an armistice with the Allies and it was then all too late.

JAPAN

At the beginning of the war, Japanese aviation capability was grossly underestimated in the West and for reasons still not clear there was a belief in London, Paris and Washington that the Japanese operated biplanes with fixed undercarriages, and that these aircraft had a short range and inferior performance. There was much evidence to the contrary but this was studiously ignored until the events of December 1941 proved those beliefs to be totally wrong, as fighters and bombers such as Mitsubishi's A6M "Zero" and G3M "Nell" were able to score astonishing successes in the early days of the Pacific war. After that, however, the United

States very rapidly produced aircraft which were greatly superior in all respects and were able to shoot the Japanese out of the sky.

Once war had started a variety of replacement aircraft programmes were set in train by the Japanese, but these new aircraft suffered a seemingly endless series of minor problems and crashes, which ensured that they were never produced in sufficient numbers to affect the war. Thus, just as the German Messerschmitt Bf 109 and Focke-Wulf Fw 190 soldiered on throughout the war, so, too, did the Japanese Navy's "Zero" and its Army equivalent, the Nakajima Ki-43 "Oscar".

SOVIET UNION

As with the Soviet Army's tanks, the Soviet Air Force was an unknown quantity at the start of the war, but it soon revealed aircraft, especially fighters and ground-attack types, which compared with the best in the world. Then the Soviets went on to produce them in such vast numbers and to use them with such disregard for casualties that the *Luftwaffe* was simply worn down in the east.

UNITED KINGDOM

The British started the war with some very ineffective aircraft, such as the Blenheim, Battle, Defiant and Gladiator, and a few excellent types, particularly the Spitfire and Hurricane. The latter two achieved immortal fame in the Battle of Britain which was the first battle in history to be fought by two air forces, without the involvement of ground troops, except for anti-aircraft gunners. The British were eventually victorious, one of the most important assets being the Rolls-Royce Merlin engine, which powered most RAF fighters and bombers, including the Hurricane, Lancaster, Mosquito, Mustang and Spitfire.

UNITED STATES

The USA termed itself the "power-house of democracy", which was certainly true where aircraft were concerned and it produced a wide range of types for the use of its own and Allied air forces and navies. Aircraft companies were among the first US institutions to come to the aid of the Allies in 1939 and, while early fighters such as the Brewster Buffalo were indifferent performers, feedback from the combat users, particularly the British RAF, resulted in rapid improvements and the appearance of world-beaters such as the North American P-51 Mustang. The United States had also long believed in the value of strategic bombing and

by the outbreak of the war had the excellent Boeing B-17 in service, while the even better B-29 was under development. The latter went on to become the first (and so far, the only) bomber to drop atomic bombs in anger and, virtually single-handedly, to bring World War II to an end in the Pacific.

NAVAL AVIATION

For the first time, naval aviation became an essential feature of modern warfare. At first carrier-borne aircraft were inferior in performance to land-based aircraft, but the Japanese "Zero" soon showed that need not be so. Soon the US Navy was operating aircraft like the Grumman F6F Hellcat and Vought F4U Corsair which were the equal of any land-based fighter and far better than anything the Japanese could put up to oppose them.

SPECIAL TYPES

Three types of aircraft both appeared and disappeared during the course of the war. The first of these was the dive-bomber, which was designed to achieve accurate bomb delivery through a near vertical descent on the target and a low-level release, followed by a sudden pull-out. The Junkers Ju 87's successes masked, at least for a time, the fact that the dive-bomber was inherently vulnerable and its day quickly passed. The second type was the turreted day fighter, which was a purely British concept and proved to be flawed; the sole machine, the Bolton-Paul Defiant, suffered disastrous losses and was quickly withdrawn. The third type was the glider, which was an attempt to insert ground troops directly onto the battlefield without the complications associated with parachute operations. Gliders were used with a degree of success in some operations, particualrly by the Germans at Eben Emäel and in Crete, and by the Americans and British at D-Day and at Arnhem. But the glider, too, suffered from a number of disadvantages and it disappeared from orders of battle from 1945 onwards.

LOSERS WHICH FOUND A DIFFERENT FIELD

Some aircraft were designed for one purpose but failed or were outclassed, but then found their value in another field. The British Bolton-Paul Defiant and the German Messerschmitt Bf 110, for example, both proved disastrous in day operations, but both became successful night fighters. Similarly, the British Fairey Swordfish started life as a torpedo-bomber but proved too slow and vulnerable, and then became a highly effective anti-submarine aircraft.

DFS 230

SPECIFICATIONS

COUNTRY OF ORIGIN: Germany.
TYPE: assault transport glider.
MANUFACTURER: DFS.
IN SERVICE: 1938-1945.
WEIGHTS: empty 1,868lb (860kg); loaded 4,630lb (2,100kg).
DIMENSIONS: span 72.0ft (22.0m); length 36.9ft (11.2m); height 9.0ft (2.7m).
PERFORMANCE: maximum gliding speed 180mph (290km/h); normal towing speed 112mph (180km/h).
WEAPONS: 1 x 7.9mm MG15 machinegun.
CREW: two.
LOAD: 8 fully-equipped troops or equivalent in stores/equipment.

DESIGN HISTORY

The German *Luftwaffe* was among the first military forces to foresee a combat role for gliders and in the mid-1930s, having observed trials of a research glider made by DFS, they ordered three for trials. This resulted in the first operational model, DFS 230A1, which was of mixed metal and wood construction, with fabric covering and high monoplane wing, supported on each side by a single brace. There was a simple, very narrow, two-wheel main undercarriage for take-off, which was then

RIGHT: *The DFS 230 on its simple two-wheel dolly, which was jettisoned after take-off, using the skid for landing. The aircraft was of mixed metal and wood construction, with fabric covering; the high wing was supported on each side by a single brace.*

BELOW: *A destroyed casemate on the Belgian fort at Eban Emäel. The top of the fort provided an excellent landing ground for gliders.*

EBEN EMÄEL: 10 MAY 1940

One of the earliest objectives on the opening day of the German attack in the West on 10 May 1940 was the Belgian fortress of Eben Emäel which dominated the crossing places on the Albert Canal. The defences were formidable and included high precipitous walls, heavily protected gun positions (two 120mm and six 75mm guns), and with anti-tank guns and machine guns covering all approaches. Hitler was shown photographs and immediately saw its weakness — the top. An attack force of paratroop engineers, commanded by Lieutenant Witzig, was selected and after intensive training they took off from Koln-Ostheim airfield at 0330 on 10 May in 11 DFS 230A1 gliders, towed by Ju 52s. En route two tow ropes snapped, one of them of the glider containing Witzig and when he landed he used the telephone number Hitler had given him for just such an emergency. Not surprisingly, a replacement Ju-52, complete with a new tow rope appeared relatively quickly and his glider was towed back into the air; he landed on Eben Emäel some three hours late.

Meanwhile, the remaining nine gliders had carried on and were cast-off at a height of some 8,000ft (2,440m) over Aachen, on the German border, as planned, from whence they glided down, seven of them landing on the roof of the fortress at 0520, taking the Belgian defenders completely by surprise. Commanded by Sergeant-Major Wenzel, the assault force, now reduced to 55 men, went into action. Among their weapons were German-developed shaped charges, which until then had been top-secret and this was their first operational use. They were employed to blast holes through the cupolas housing the 75mm guns, although the 120mm turrets proved too tough, and the guns had to be destroyed by pushing charges down the

barrels and then detonating them.

The problem for the defenders was that the turrets were unable to support each other and no weapons were sited to clear attackers off the top of the fortress. Thus, the attackers were able to defeat the turrets one at a time and then to gain access to the interior where they defeated the Belgians in their isolated groups. At a cost of six men killed and 20 wounded, Witzig and his men defeated a force almost 1,000 strong and captured a fortress considered to be "impregnable".

This was the first combat use of assault gliders and proved a triumphant success, resulting in the expansion of German glider forces and the rapid creation of new glider forces in Britain and the United States.

jettisoned. The glider landed on a single, central skid. There was also a simple tail-skid.

The DFS 230 could be towed by a variety of Luftwaffe aircraft, usually the Heinkel He 46 or Henschel Hs 126, both single-engined aircraft originally employed on battlefield reconnaissance and army cooperation duties. The tri-motor Junkers Ju 52 was also used.

The major problem for the DFS 230A1 occurred during the final approach and landing, when the passengers were confined to their seats and unable to return ground fire. This led to the development of a new version, DFS 230B1, with a braking parachute which deployed from a small tube under the tail. There were parallel dual-control trainers, designated DFS 230A2 and DFS 230B2, respectively. A later version, DFS 230C1, also had forward-facing rockets, which not only acted as brakes but also emitted a dense cloud of smoke, thus masking the aircraft from accurate hostile fire. Another version had autogiro blades, but although tested it was not proceeded with.

ABOVE: *DFS 230s were towed at 112mph (180km/h) and, like all gliders, were very vulnerable when under tow and coming in to land.*

BELOW: *An Allied officer examines a DFS 230 in the North African desert. After the attack on Eben Emäel the DFS-230 was never a total success.*

SPECIFICATIONS

COUNTRY OF ORIGIN: Germany.

TYPE: single-seat fighter-bomber.

MANUFACTURER: Focke-Wulf Flugzeugbau.

IN SERVICE: 1941–1945.

WEIGHTS: empty 7,055lb (3,200kg); max take-off 10,800lb (4,900kg).

DIMENSIONS: span 34.5ft (10.5m); length 29.0ft (8.8m); height 13.0ft (4.0m).

ENGINE: 1 x BMW 801Dg 18-cylinder, two-row radial, 1,700hp (2,100hp emergency boost).

PERFORMANCE: max speed (with boost) 408mph (653km/h); initial climb 2,350ft/min (720m/min); service ceiling 37,400ft (11,410m); range on internal fuel about 560 miles (900km).

WEAPONS: 2 x 13mm MG 131 above engine; 2 x 20mm MG 151/20 in wing roots; 2 x MG 151/20 or 30mm MK 108 in outer wings.

FOCKE-WULF
Fw 190A-8

DESIGN HISTORY

The Fw 190 was conceived as the first of the second generation of monoplane fighters (Bf 109 being the first) and the first prototype flew on 1 June 1939, just before the outbreak of war. The British were unaware of its existence until the first squadrons were met in combat over France in early 1941 and little detail was known until an Fw 190A-3 landed in error in England. Tests on this showed that the German aircraft was superior to British contemporary fighters in many respects, being faster, better armed, stronger, more manoeuvrable and lighter. The Fw 190 was produced in large numbers (20,051) in many factories, but it never totally supplanted the Bf 109.

ABOVE: Focke-Wulf Fw 190-A8 in the colours of II/JG 11 at Darmstadt, in early 1945, with the yellow "Eastern Front" theatre band.

OPERATION DONNERKEIL: 12 FEBRUARY 1941

The ship element of the "Channel Dash" (Operation *Cerberus*) is described elsewhere; the provision of continuous air cover by the *Luftwaffe*, Operation *Donnerkeil* (thunderbolt), was an essential element of that success. This was planned by the fighter general, Adolf Galland, and involved continuous air cover for the ships from leaving Brest to their arrival in German waters.

Galland divided the route into three sectors and exercised command from ashore, but with a senior *Luftwaffe* officer accompanied by a communications team aboard *Scharnhorst*; night fighters covered the periods of darkness at the start and end of the voyage. Daylight cover was provided by *Jagdgruppen* (fighter groups) equipped with 252 Fw 190As and Bf 109Fs from *Jagdgeschwader* (fighter squadrons) *JG.1, 2* and *26*, and training units mobilised for this operation.

Galland devised a system of rolling cover in which groups of 16 aircraft each provided 30 minutes of low-level cover over the ships, with the next group arriving 10 minutes before its scheduled takeover time. In this way, for 20 minutes in every hour there were actually 32 aircraft overhead. Having been relieved, each group then went to a new airfield further along the coast, thus increasing the numbers available as the ships reached the area of maximum threat in and beyond the Straits of Dover.

Incredibly, this was achieved in complete radio silence, although the game was nearly given away when British radars spotted the aircraft circling and moving slowly eastwards long before they spotted the ships below them. However, it took some time for the significance to be realised, and even then there were extraordinary delays within the British chain-of-command before it responded. Just as one of the *Luftwaffe* group changeovers was taking place at 1300 on 12 February the first serious British attack was carried out by six antiquated Swordfish torpedo-bombers escorted by 11 Spitfires, but this was quickly dealt with by the German fighters, their main problem being the 90kt speed of the Swordfish, which forced

TOP: *Fw 190-A3 in the air, showing the troughs for the twin 7.92mm MG17 machine guns ahead of the cockpit. There were also two 20mm cannon in each wing.*

RIGHT: *Cockpit of a Focke-Wulf Fw 190A-4, introduced in mid-1942. Powered by a water-injected BMW 801D-2 engine its top speed was 416mph (617km/h).*

some German pilots to lower their undercarriages to reduce their speed. All six Swordfish were destroyed, either by the fighters or by anti-aircraft fire from the ships.

With this British attack, Galland lifted radio silence, but by then *Scharnhorst*, *Gneisenau* and *Prinz Eugen* warships were through the Straits of Dover and within range of even more *Luftwaffe* bases in Belgium and the Netherlands, enabling him to add a further sixteen aircraft at a somewhat higher level. This enhanced air escort dealt with the remaining uncoordinated and sporadic RAF attacks with ease.

The Luftwaffe operation was a complete success and, most importantly, the only damage to any of the three big ships came when *Scharnhorst* hit a mine off the Dutch coast. In achieving protective success, the *Luftwaffe* destroyed 41 British aircraft for a loss of 17 fighters and five bombers (two of which collided with each other) and a total of 23 men. It was a triumph in which the Fw 190 played the leading role and an event which Galland personally considered to have been his greatest achievement.

SPECIFICATIONS

COUNTRY OF ORIGIN: Germany.

TYPE: tactical transport.

MANUFACTURER: Junkers Flugzeug und Motorenwerke.

IN SERVICE: 1935–1945.

WEIGHTS: empty 14,462lb (6,560kg); max take-off 23,180lb (10,515kg).

DIMENSIONS: span 96.0ft (29.3m); length 62.0ft (18.8m); height 14.8ft (4.5m).

ENGINES: 3 x BMW 132T-2 nine-cylinder radials; each 830hp.

PERFORMANCE: max speed at sea level 183mph (295km/h); initial climb 680ft/min (208m/min); service ceiling 18,045ft (5,500m); range about 800 miles (1,290km).

WEAPONS: typically, one 7.92mm MG15 machine gun in dorsal position, two 7.92mm machine guns firing through cabin windows.

CREW: 3 (pilot, co-pilot, radio operator).

PAYLOAD: 18 passengers or freight.

JUNKERS JU 52/3MG3E

DESIGN HISTORY

The Ju 52 was a single-engined transport which first flew in 1930, but following the fashion of the day it was adapted by the addition of two more engines. With three Pratt & Whitney Hornet engines of 525hp each, it was designated Ju 52/3m (3m = *drei Motoren* = three engines). This first flew in April 1932 and immediately found numerous civilian customers. In 1934 a military bomber/transport version, Junkers Ju 32/3mg3e, appeared, which carried six 220lb (100kg) bombs and had two turrets, one dorsal the other ventral, each mounting a single 7.92mm machine gun. This was immediately ordered in large numbers by the newly formed *Luftwaffe*, but despite its bombing capability, it was almost always employed as a transport, although those sent to support Franco in the Spanish Civil War did occasionally carry out bombing raids. As a transport, it had two rows of nine inward-facing seats. The original military model had two

ABOVE: *This Junkers Ju 52/3m has managed to land at Maleme airfield during the attack on Crete and discharges its load of Alpine troops of 5th Mountain Division. These tough troops were serving on this occasion in the air-mobile role.*

RIGHT: *During the battle for Crete, pilots of Ju 52/3ms were ordered to deliver the troops at all costs and this aircraft has crash-landed, stopping just short of a brick wall. Even so, it still managed to deliver its passengers safely.*

mainwheels with wheel fairings (which were almost invariably removed by operational crews) and a tailskid, later replaced by a tailwheel. There was also a version with skis and another on floats.

BELOW: *A British air photograph of Maleme airfield, taken during a raid, showing eleven Ju 52/3ms on the ground, most of them badly damaged, as well as several DFS-230 gliders. Note the bomb explosions among the aircraft on the left and another direct hit lower right.*

INVASION OF CRETE: MAY 1941

The German airborne assault on Crete, a mountainous island in the eastern Mediterranean, was led by *Luftwaffe* General Student, commander of German airborne troops,* and involved two paratroop formations, 7th Airborne Division and the Airborne Assault Regiment, plus 5th Mountain Division, employed in the air-mobile role. The air transport allocated to the operation comprised some 500 Junkers Ju 52/3m and 72 DFS 230 gliders.

The island of Crete is some 179 miles (290km) long and 20-30 miles (32-48km) wide, with a central mountainous ridge descending sharply to the sea in the south, but with a narrow coastal strip to the north. In 1940 this plain contained the only significant towns, ports and roads, as well as three airfields, at Maleme, Restina and Heraklion. The defending troops, some 32,000 British Commonwealth and 14,000 Greeks, had all recently abandoned Greece and were short of all military weapons, equipment and supplies.

The German attack was preceded by several days of air attacks and then, on 20 May, the gliderborne landing commenced. Two companies landed near Maleme and Canea airfields, although two other glider landings were complete failures. The paratroops arrived 15 minutes after the gliders and this, too, was a near-disaster, with many men descending straight on to Allied positions, most being either killed or wounded. The second wave was delayed and when it arrived in

the late afternoon the men were heavily attacked by Allied troops. Despite these setbacks, by the end of the first day 8,000 paratroops and 750 glider troops were on the ground.

Next day more paratroops jumped in with complete disregard for casualties and gained control of sufficient parts of Maleme airfield for Student to despatch elements of 5th Mountain Division by Ju 52/3m, whose pilots were instructed to land at all costs. Many Ju 52/3ms were shot down with heavy loss of life, but sufficient landed (some in semi-controlled crashes) to enable the Germans to hold the airfield. Despite heavy losses the fly-in continued and by the end of the battle 15,000 men and 750 vehicles had passed through the airfield. The fighting continued over the next few days, but the Germans pushed the Allied forces back and a seaborne evacuation started, ending on 31 May. The British lost 5,490 killed and 11,835 captured, while the Germans lost 5,670 men. Of the 530 Ju 52s involved, 170 were either shot down or badly damaged.

The Ju 52/3m was slow and unglamorous, with a maximum load of 18 men, but it delivered just enough men and stores to Crete to make victory possible, although at such cost that Goering's vaunted parachute troops were never again used in an air assault.

---

* In the German armed forces of the Third Reich the Fallschirmjäger (paratroops) belonged to the Luftwaffe (air force), not to the army.

JUNKERS JU 87B-1 "STUKA"

SPECIFICATIONS

COUNTRY OF ORIGIN: Germany.

TYPE: two-seat dive-bomber/ground-attack.

MANUFACTURER: Junkers Flugzeugbau und Motorenwerke AG.

IN SERVICE: 1938–1945.

WEIGHTS: empty 6,080lb (2,750kg); loaded 9,371lb (4,250kg).

DIMENSIONS: span 45.3ft (13.8); length 36.4ft (11.1m); height 12.8ft (3.9m).

ENGINE: 1 x Junkers Jumo 211Da 12-cylinder, inverted-vee, liquid-cooled; 1,100hp.

PERFORMANCE: max speed 242mph (390km/h); service ceiling 26,250ft (8,000m); range with max bomb load, 373 miles (600km).

WEAPONS: 2 x 7.92mm MG17 machine guns in wings, one 7.92mm MG manually operated in rear cockpit; one 1,102lb (500kg) bomb (centreline) and four 110lb (50kg) bombs (underwing racks).

DESIGN HISTORY

The prototype Ju 87 flew in 1935 and the type entered production in 1937 as the Ju 87A, powered by a Jumo 210 engine and with a large trousered undercarriage. It was fully equipped for dive-bombing, which included an aiming system and a heavy crutch that swung the 1,102lb (500kg) bomb well clear of the fuselage and propeller before release. Early experience led to a number of improvements including a much more powerful Jumo 211 engine and an alteration in the undercarriage streamlining from "trousers" to "spats" and a large "cowl". This version was designated the Ju 87B1 and was the type in service at the outbreak of World War II.

ABOVE: *The personal Ju 87D-1 Trop of commander Stukageschwader 3, based at Derna, Libya in June 1942.*

BELOW: *France, May 1940. Groundcrew wind the Ju 87's inertia starter before a flight across the English Channel*

BELOW: *A large group of Ju 87s on its way to attack British 8th Army units in the Western Desert in November 1941. Even at this stage of the war the Ju 87 was out-of-date and very vulnerable.*

BELOW RIGHT: *Ju 87 with an escorting Bf 109. After its triumphs in Poland (1939) and France (1940), the Stuka needed to be escorted by fighters if there was to be a reasonable hope of survival.*

INVASION OF POLAND: SEPTEMBER 1939

The Ju 87 made its debut in the Spanish Civil War, but it was its performance in Poland that established the type's terrifying reputation. A formation of three Ju 87s carried out the first bombing attack of World War II when, on the opening day of the campaign, three aircraft of *3/St.G1* attacked Polish positions near the Dirschau bridges across the river Vistula. Thereafter the Ju 87s combined with the *panzers* on the ground to establish *blitzkrieg* (literally, lightning war) as a new way of waging war. Nowhere did new and old appear in starker contrast than in the unique confrontation when Ju 87s attacked and annihilated a Polish horse cavalry brigade at Wielum.

With total air superiority, the Ju 87s were able to roam the skies of Poland at will, attacking whatever targets offered themselves. Apart from the 500kg (1,102lb) centre-line bomb they also used 50kg (110lb) fragmentation bombs to great effect, and when those had been used up they went down to low level and used their wing-mounted machine guns.

The final phase of the campaign was the defence of Warsaw, but on 15 September the *Luftwaffe* started a massive attack on the doomed capital, employing some 400 aircraft, of which 240 were Ju 87s. High-level bombers dropped high-explosive bombs, the Ju 87s incendiaries and the Poles surrendered on 27 September.

The Ju 87s repeated this success in Greece, Crete and the early parts of the Russian campaign, but during the Battle of Britain the squadrons suffered such heavy losses that they had to be withdrawn. The Ju 87 went on to become a feared anti-ship aircraft, but from 1942 onwards its primary deployment was to the Eastern Front, where it was used mainly as a "tank-buster" armed with two large 37mm cannon in underwing pods.

The Ju 87 was instantly recognisable from its ungainly appearance, cranked wings, large fixed undercarriage and its characteristic mode of attack. The control system was very simple, the pilot having a set of aiming lines painted on the cockpit canopy and while dives sometimes were at 90 degrees, it was more usual for them to be at an angle of between 70 degrees and 85 degrees. In the dive, wing-mounted brakes were deployed to ensure that the aircraft did not exceed the maximum safe dive speed of 375mph (604km/h) and immediately following release the pilot pulled back on the stick. One early problem was that the pilot sometimes blacked-out and lost control, which happened on several occasions in the Spanish Civil War; indeed, on one occasion a whole formation was late in pulling out over misty ground and many of the aircraft simply flew into the ground. This problem was solved by fitting a rudimentary form of auto-pilot.

One feature which caught the popular imagination was the result of experience in Spain, where it was observed that when the aircraft was in the dive its high-pitched engine whine, coupled with the whistle of the falling bomb, had a terrorising effect on people on the ground. This effect was deliberately enhanced by fitting a propeller-driven siren on the port undercarriage leg. In the early days of World War II, the Ju 87 was so effective that the German generic name for a dive bomber, *Sturzkampfflugzeug* (normally abbreviated to *Stuka),* came to be applied exclusively to the Ju 87.

SPECIFICATIONS

COUNRY OF ORIGIN: Germany.
TYPE: single-seat fighter.
MANUFACTURER: Bayrische Flugzeugwerke (renamed Messerschmitt AG in 1938).
IN SERVICE: 1943-43.
WEIGHTS: empty 4,189lb (1,900kg); max take-off 6,100lb (2,767kg).
DIMENSIONS: span 32.38ft (9.87m); length 28.35ft (8.64m); height 7.55ft (2.3m).
ENGINE: 1 x Daimler-Benz DB 601N inverted vee-12, liquid-cooled, in-line, 1,200hp.
PERFORMANCE: max speed 354mph (570km/h) at 12,305ft (3,750m); initial climb 3,280ft/min (1,000m/min); service ceiling 34,450ft (10,500m); range about 365–460 miles (585–735km).
WEAPONS: 1 x 20mm cannon (propeller hub); four 7.9mm MG 17 machine gun (two in nose, two in wing).
(Specifications for Bf 109E7)

MESSERSCHMITT BF 109E

DESIGN HISTORY

The Bf 109 was one of the greatest fighters in aviation history. First flown in 1935, early versions gained valuable experience in the Spanish Civil War and by the time World War II started the major production version was the Bf 190E, known throughout the *Luftwaffe* as the *"Emil"* (from the German phonetic alphabet).

The Bf 109 was a low-wing monoplane fighter, the early versions being powered by a JuMo engine with a two-bladed propeller, but the *"Emil"* introduced the Daimler-Benz DB 601 inverted-vee, 12-cylinder engine with direct fuel-injection and a three-bladed propeller, which combined to give improved dive characteristics and better fuel

LEFT: *An "Emil" escorts a Ju 57 Stuka over the desert. By 1942 fighter escorts were essential as the British knew exactly how to deal with the lumbering dive-bomber.*

ABOVE: *Bf 109E-4/Trop of JG 27. Note the* gruppe *insignia on the nose, the extended sand filter on the engine air intake — and the ground crew's pith helmets!*

LEFT: *This Bf 109E4 flew with I/JG1 at De Kooy, Netherlands in 1941. The main advantages of the Bf 109 were its small size, high acceleration and good manoeuvrability, coupled with cheap, rapid production.*

NORTH AFRICA: JANUARY–SEPTEMBER 1942

The Bf 109 served the *Luftwaffe* from the first to last days of World War II. Just over 200 took part in invasion of Poland, of which 67 were lost, most to ground AA fire, and a much greater number took part in the invasion of France and the Low Countries, before switching to the daylight battles over Britain. In many cases, battle-experienced Bf 109 pilots proved superior to RAF Hurricane pilots and in some cases to those of Spitfires as well, but they had insufficient fuel to stay over the operational area for more than a few minutes, and their effectiveness was further impaired by Goering's order that they had to serve as close escorts to the bomber formations, since the Bf 110 had proved a disaster.

After the Battle of Britain, the Bf 109 served in all German theatres of war, but a campaign in which it left a particular mark was the North African desert, where Bf 109Es formed *Jagdgruppe* (fighter group) 27 (*JG.27*), part of *Fliegerkorps Afrika* supporting Rommel's *Afrika Korps*. For some months the German fighters achieved numerous successes against the Desert Air Force's Hurricanes and early model Curtis P-40s, and German *experten* (aces) built up impressive scores. Indeed, some observers noted that the issue of "victories" came to dominate German fighter pilots' motivation, to the extent that they concentrated their efforts into a private war against British fighters and left the bombers and reconnaissance aircraft alone.

JG.27 included a large number of *experten* in its ranks, of whom the most famous was *Leutnant* Hans-Joachim Marseille, the Luftwaffe's top-scoring fighter pilot in the West. He had flown in the Battle of Britain, although without particularly distinguishing himself, but that changed dramatically in the

ABOVE: *Hans-Joachim Marseille was a natural fighter pilot, once shooting down 12 enemy aircraft in a day. He died on 30 September, 1942; his final score was 158.*

economy. The Bf 109's good points included its small size, low cross-section, high acceleration, fast climb and dive, and excellent manoeuvrability, coupled with rapid and cheap production. It also suffered from a number of drawbacks, including relatively poor visibility for the pilot, narrow landing gear, severe swing on take-off/landing, poor lateral control at high speeds and the fact that the automatic wing-slats often opened in tight turns or in the slip-stream of an intended victim, thoroughly upsetting the pilot's aim. Bf 109Es were fitted with either two or three 20mm cannon, which had an effective range and striking power far greater than the battery of eight 0.303in machine guns used in British fighters such as Spitfire and Hurricane.

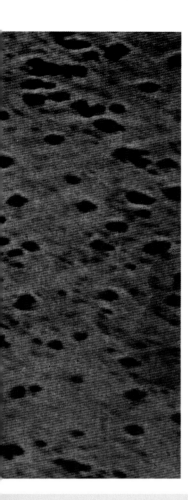

LEFT: *A Messerschmitt Bf 109E-4/Trop of II/JG 27. One Bf 109 of this squadron shot down an RAF transport carrying Lt-Gen Gott, the newly appointed Commander 8th Army. That death resulted in the arrival of an obscure officer from England to take Gott's place: his name – Bernard Montgomery.*

RIGHT: *The cockpit of a Bf 109-E4/ Trop, which makes an interesting comparison with that of the Fw 190 on page 57. It was not the place for tall or plump pilots!*

North African skies. He downed his fortieth victim in February 1942 and by June had taken his "score" to 102. He was an excellent marksman, seemed to have a natural flair for deflection shooting, and was also parsimonious with ammunition. His personal best score was 12 enemy aircraft in one day.

On 7 August 1942, however, *Unteroffizier* Schneider of II/27 was on an offensive sweep when he had a chance encounter with an RAF transport, a Bristol Bombay, which was bumbling along at low level. Seizing his opportunity, he shot it down in flames, killing all the crew and passengers. The most important of those passengers was the newly promoted Lieutenant-General Gott on his way to take command of the British 8th Army, and Schneider thus changed the course of military history, since Gott was replaced by a hitherto unknown officer from England, Lieutenant-General Montgomery.

In September 1942 *JG.27's* Bf 109Es found themselves opposed by Spitfire Vs and P-40Fs whose pilots had evolved tactics to overcome the Bf 109E's superiority. In that month *JG.27* lost 15 pilots, including *Leutnant* Stahlschmitt (59 victories), *Oberfeldwebel* Steinhausen (40 victories) and *Leutnant* von Lieres (24 victories). The worst blow, however, came on 30 September when Marseille, whose personal score had risen to 158, was flying a new Bf 109G and engine trouble led to the cockpit filling with smoke. Marseille was killed trying to bale out.

The Bf 109 was the workhorse of the *Luftwaffe's* fighter units and always did well in combat with the Allies. It achieved periods of supremacy, such as in Poland and in North Africa up to September 1942, but it seldom triumphed absolutely.

MITSUBISHI A6M2 ZERO-SEN ("ZEKE")

DESIGN HISTORY

The Imperial Japanese Navy (IJN) A6M's original name was "Reisen" and its Allied reporting name was "Zeke" but it achieved undying fame under its designation of "Zero", taken from the last digit of the Japanese year of its introduction into service. Its appearance came as a very unpleasant surprise to American and British staffs on the outbreak of the Pacific War, who appear to have ignored its successes in the war in China, despite warnings from American volunteer pilots flying for the Chinese.

BELOW: *A later version of Japan's famous fighter – the Mitsubishi A6M5 Model 52.*

SPECIFICATIONS

COUNTRY OF ORIGIN: Japan.
TYPE: single-seat carrier-borne fighter.
MANUFACTURER: Mitsubishi Jukogyo KK.
IN SERVICE: 1940–1945.
WEIGHTS: empty 3,704lb (1,680kg); max loaded 5,313lb (2,410kg).
DIMENSIONS: span 39.3ft (12.0m); length 29.8ft (9.1m); height 9.6ft (3.0m).
ENGINE: 1 x Nakajima NK1C Sakae 21 14-cylinder two-row radial air-cooled supercharged; 925hp.
PERFORMANCE: max speed 316mph (509km/h); initial climb 4,500ft/min (1,370m/min); ceiling 33,790ft (10,300m); range with drop tanks 1,940 miles (3,110km).
WEAPONS: 2 x 20mm Type 99 MG (wings); 2 x 7.7mm (0.303in) Type 97 MG (fuselage); wing rack for 2 x 66lb (30kg) bombs.

The IJN set severe demands in its 1937 operational requirement, including 500km/h (311mph) top speed and a weapons fit of two cannon and two machine guns. The prototype flew on 1 April 1939, two squadrons were deployed to China in July 1940 where they eliminated all opposition, and some 400 had been delivered by the time the first production version, A6M2, and the clipped-wing A6M3 appeared over Pearl Harbor and the Philippines on 7 December 1941.

The Zero had unrivalled manoeuverability and excellent range, all achieved with a comparatively small engine and 182 gallons (827 litres) of fuel in internal and two drop tanks. For a time the Japanese people believed that the "Zero" was invincible, although after the Battle of Midway the Allies began to gain the upper hand with aircraft such as the F4U and F6F.

ATTACK ON CLARK FIELD, PHILIPPINES: 7 DECEMBER 1941.

Although overshadowed by the Pearl Harbor success, the attack on the Philippines was as dramatic. Japan's six big carriers were required for the Hawaii attack, while the three smaller carriers could not carry sufficient aircraft to attack US bases in the Philippines, especially Clark Field, some 75 miles (120km) North of Manila. Japan had bases on Formosa (modern Taiwan), which was within bomber range, but seemed to be outside that of fighters, until the imagination and flying skills of the IJN's pilots provided the answer by virtually doubling the range of their "Zeroes". The "Zero's" fuel capacity (internal tanks plus two wing tanks) was fixed at 182 gallons (827 litres), while normal consumption rate was 35 gallons (159 litres) per hour. However, by repeated training it was found that pilots could reduce fuel consumption to 17 gallons (77 litres) per hour by cruising at 115kts (185km/h) at 12,000ft (3,660m) with propeller revolutions at 1,700–1,800 rpm. This required great skill and patience, since the aircraft was just above stalling speed, but gave the range to fly from Formosa, operate at full power during the attacks on US airfields, and then return to Formosa.

It had been hoped to hit the Philippine targets at dawn, but dense fog over Formosa caused a five hour delay, which the Japanese thought would result in either an air raid by Boeing B-17 bombers against their airfields in Formosa or in the US air forces in the Philippines being ready to resist their attack. In the event neither happened. US commanders in the Philippines had received news of the Pearl Harbor attack, but there was then a period of confusion and indecision. The USAAF commander

ordered the aircraft at Clark Field to take-off to avoid being attacked on the ground. However, first, the P-40 fighters had to land because of lack of fuel and, secondly, the B-17s were recalled to bomb-up for an attack on Formosa, which meant that virtually all Clark Field's aircraft were on the ground when the Japanese arrived.

There were some 200 Japanese aircraft in three waves, the first arriving just before 1200. A very few P-40s managed to scramble but were overwhelmed by the sheer numbers of "Zeroes". In the whole of that day the Japanese lost seven fighters but all bombers returned unscathed to Taiwan; the US, however, lost 18 B-17s and over 50 fighters, plus hangars, radars, radio stations and other ground facilities. It was a smashing victory for the Japanese, made possible by the skill of the "Zero" pilots in nursing so many extra miles out of their "Zeroes".

BELOW LEFT: *The "Zero" came as a sharp surprise to the Allies who had seriously under-rated Japanese abilities.*

ABOVE RIGHT: *A single long-range tank gave these A6M3 Model 22 fighters a radius of some 650 miles.*

BELOW: *The end of the road for a* kamikaze *pilot as he taxis his Zero out for take-off for his final flight.*

RIGHT: *Zero takes off later in the war, by which time it was completely outclassed by new US fighters.*

MITSUBISHI G3M2 ("NELL")

SPECIFICATIONS

COUNTRY OF ORIGIN: Japan.

TYPE: land-based, long-range bomber.

MANUFACTURER: Mitsubishi Jukogyo KK.

IN SERVICE: 1937–1943.

WEIGHTS: empty 10,516lb (4,770kg); max loaded 16,848lb (7,642kg).

DIMENSIONS: span 82.0ft (25.0m); length 54.0ft (16.5m); height 12.0ft (3.7m).

ENGINE: 2 x Mitsubishi Kinsei-3 14-cylinder, two-row, air-cooled radials, each 910hp.

PERFORMANCE: max speed 2325mph (373km/h); service ceiling 33,730ft (7,640m); range 3,871 miles (6,228km).

WEAPONS: 4 x 7.7mm Type 92 MG (dorsal/ventral/cockpit position).

BOMBS: 1 x 18in (457mm) torpedo or 3 x 551lb (25kg) bombs.

CREW: seven.

DESIGN HISTORY

The Mitsubishi G3M (US reporting name "Nell") first flew in July 1935 in answer to an Imperial Japanese Navy requirement for a very long-range, land-based bomber. It was a smooth, stressed-skin monoplane, powered by two 910hp Mitsubishi radial engines. Payload comprised either a single torpedo carried externally or a number of bombs carried in an internal bomb bay. The G3M entered service in late 1936 and by 1943 it had been relegated to second-line duties. A total of 1,048 were produced.

ABOVE: *A formation of Mitsubishi G3M3 bombers with dorsal turrets extended. G3M3s were the main part of the force that sank the British* battleship Prince of Wales *and battlecruiser* Repulse *in a short and sharp engagement which seriously dented British naval pride.*

RIGHT: *The British suffered a great blow when, without air cover,* HMS Prince of Wales *(seen at Singapore) and* Repulse *were sunk by Japanese "Nell" and "Betty" bombers.*

SINKING *PRINCE OF WALES/REPULSE*: 10 DECEMBER 1941

The G3M2's greatest moment came on 10 December 1941. Japanese amphibious forces landed on the north Malayan coast on 7 December 1941 and immediately started driving south overland. Japanese naval commanders were, however, concerned about the two British capital ships, battleship *Prince of Wales* (35,000 tons) and battlecruiser Repulse (32,000 tons), which they knew had recently arrived in Singapore. Such ships could easily interfere seriously with Japanese operations and numerous aerial reconnaissances were undertaken on 8 and 9 December to find them. The first report was that "two battleships, four cruisers and four destroyers" were at anchor in Singapore, but on the afternoon of 9 December a Japanese submarine radioed a report that it had seen two battleships at sea, heading northwards.

At this stage the initial Japanese landings in north-east Malaya had been completed and the task force was heading back for Cam Ranh Bay on the coast of Indochina, but on receipt of the submarine report the Japanese naval commander sent the troop ships to shelter in the Gulf of Siam and launched floatplanes to seek the British ships.

Aircraft of 22nd Air Flotilla, based on airfields around Saigon, had bombed Singapore on 8 December and Kuantan on 9 December and were back at base when news was received of the submarine sighting. Some 95 aircraft immediately took off to attack the British ships (some 30 G4M1 "Betty" and 60 G3M1 "Nell") but when darkness fell and they had not found the British ships they returned to base. At 0340 the following morning, however, another sighting report was received and the aircraft took off for a second attempt. They reached the southern limit of their flight without seeing their target and had turned northwards again when they spotted the British force (*Prince of*

Wales, *Repulse* and four destroyers) and immediately went into the attack.

First was a high-level bombing attack from 10,000ft (3,000m) against *Repulse* which was hit once with little damage. Approximately half-an-hour later a squadron of torpedo bombers attacked, dropping their "fish" from a height of 3-400ft (90–120m) and a range of approximately 1,500 yards (1,400m). Two scored hits on *Prince of Wales*, reducing its speed to 15knots, but *Repulse* took successful evasive action. A second torpedo attack and a second bombing attack failed to score any hits on either ship, but a third torpedo attack was put in at 1222 in which several hits were scored on *Repulse* slowing it dramatically. Then yet another attack brought the wounded ship to a halt and the crew abandoned ship just before it rolled over and sank.

The Japanese aircraft now concentrated on the *Prince of Wales* and a bomb tore into her innards before exploding. The end came only a few minutes later. The British lost a battleship and a battlecruiser and 840 men, including Admiral Phillips and the captain of the *Prince of Wales*, while Japanese losses were three aircraft and 21 crewmen.

To the astonishment of the Japanese, the British ships had no air cover, the carrier *Illustrious* which should have been part of Force Z being under repair in the United States, while no land-based aircraft were made available. The G3M1 "Nell" (supported by G4M1 "Betty") played the predominant role in this undoubted Japanese triumph, although it proved to be short-lived, since the Allies soon realised the dominance of air power in naval battles and over the next three-and-a-half years used it to annihilate the IJN fleet.

NAKAJIMA B5N2 ("KATE")

DESIGN HISTORY

The Nakajima B5N ("Kate") was designed to meet a 1935 Japanese Navy requirement, and, for its day, it was an advanced and bold design, with stressed skin, variable-pitch propeller, hydraulically retracting undercarriage, Fowler flaps, NACA cowling and integral wing fuel tanks. It even had hydraulic wing-folding – the first in any navy – although this was found to be troublesome and deleted. The challenging specification demanded a speed of 205mph (330km/h) but the prototype beat this by 23mph (37km/h). The B5N1 went into service in 1937 but by 1941 it was approaching obsolescence, although 103 took part in the Pearl Harbor attack. An improved version, designated B5N2, entered service in early 1941; this had a more

powerful engine, which increased speed and ceiling, although at the cost of reduced range. Forty of these took part in the Pearl Harbor attack.

SPECIFICATIONS
COUNTRY OF ORIGIN: Japan.
TYPE: three-seat carrier-borne torpedo-bomber.
MANUFACTURER: Nakajima Hikoki KK.
IN SERVICE: 1939–1945.
WEIGHTS: empty 5,024lb (2,279kg); max loaded 9,039lb (4,100kg).
DIMENSIONS: span 50.9ft (15.5m); length 33.8ft (10.3m); height 12.1ft (3.7m).
ENGINE: 1 x Nakajima Sakae 21 14-cylinder two-row radial air-cooled; 1,115hp.
PERFORMANCE: max speed 235mph (378km/h); initial climb 1,378ft/min (420m/min); ceiling 25,000ft (7,640m); range 1,238 miles (2,000km).
WEAPONS: 2 x 7.7mm MG (rear cockpit, flexible mount); 2 x 7.7mm MG (forward firing, fixed mount); 1 x 18in (457mm) torpedo or 3 x 551lb (25kg) bombs.

PEARL HARBOR: 7 DECEMBER 1941

The air attack on Pearl Harbor was carried out by 145 B5N1 and B5N2 "Kates", 105 as high-level bombers and 40 as torpedo bombers); 131 D3A1 "Vals" (all dive-bombers) and 79 A6M "Zero" fighters, which were split into two waves. They took off from aircraft carriers at 0600 on Sunday 7 December and flow some 275mm southwards. As the first wave passed over the northern tip of Oahu, the B5N "Kates" split away so that they would approach the target from the south, while the "Val" dive-bombers and "Zero" fighters attacked the airfields. As they approached their targets, the torpedo-armed B5Ns dropped to low-level, before splitting into two groups to attack the ships in the harbour from opposite directions, the first strike being delivered at 0753.

The US battleships were moored in "Battleship Row" on the eastern side of Ford Island and within minutes four were ablaze and sinking. *Arizona* blew up and split into two, *Oklahoma* turned over, *West Virginia* sank and *California*'s fuel tanks were set alight and burned for three days, until it, too, sank. *Nevada* managed to get under way but was forced to beach, but *Maryland, Tennessee* and *Pennsylvania* were left virtually unscathed. The other Japanese aim was to destroy as many aircraft as possible and aircraft attacked Kaneohe flying-boat base (27 out of 36 Catalinas destroyed) and Ewa Field (33 out of 49 aircraft destroyed). Other aircraft attacked the remaining airfields, and when the first wave departed to return to the Japanese carriers they had lost just nine of their number.

The second wave arrived at 0845 and attacked the same targets, although the targets hit were fewer and the losses greater. There should also have been a third wave, but this was cancelled by the task group commander, Vice-Admiral Nagumo.

The Japanese aircraft performed their missions very well, inflicting heavy losses on enemy ships and targets. Their own losses were much fewer, comprising 15 D3A1 "Vals", nine A6M "Zeroes" and five B5N "Kate" torpedo-bombers (no B5N high-level bombers were lost). Nevertheless, as described elsewhere, the major aim – the destruction of the US aircraft-carriers) was not achieved, while the destruction of the oil tanks by the cancelled third wave would have added greatly to the scope of the victory. The Japanese had learnt well from the British victory at Taranto and the B5N "Kate", and, in particular the torpedo-bombers, had played a crucial role in that success.

LEFT: *The Nakajima B5N2 Kate's Type 91 torpedo was usually released at 250ft (76m) but at Pearl Harbor it had to be dropped from a much lower height and was fitted with a special wooden tailplane for extra control.*

ABOVE RIGHT: *The result of the Kate's endeavours as the battleship, USS* Arizona, *burns fiercely in Pearl Harbor.*

BELOW: *The B5N2 ('Kate') was the IJN torpedo-bomber in the Pearl Harbor operation.*

In its torpedo-bomber role, the B5N2 carried the 17.7in (450mm) Type 91 torpedo, which was released at 250ft (76m) and 280mph (402km/h), and normally entered the water at a steep angle before setting course for the target at a speed of 45kt. These factors resulted in a less dangerous launch profile than for the contemporary British Swordfish, but at Pearl Harbor the targets were in shallow water, so that the torpedoes had to be fitted with a wooden "air tail" and released from a lower height.

YAKOVLEV YAK-3

SPECIFICATIONS
COUNTYR OF ORIGIN: Soviet Union.
TYPE: single-seat fighter.
MANUFACTURER: design bureau of A.S. Yakovlev.
IN SERVICE: 1943–1945.
WEIGHTS: empty 4,960lb (2,250kg); loaded 5,864lb (2,660kg).
DIMENSIONS: span 30.2ft (9.2m); length 27.9ft (8.5m); height 7.8ft (2.4m).
ENGINE: 1 x Klimov VK-107A V-12 liquid-cooled; 1,650hp.
PERFORMANCE: max speed 404mph (650km/h); initial climb 5,250ft/min (1,600m/min); service ceiling 35,450ft (10,800m); range about 506 miles (815km).
WEAPONS: 1 x 20m ShVAK cannon (120 rounds), 2 x 12.7mm BS MG (each 250 rounds).

DESIGN HISTORY

Like other elements of the German armed forces, the *Luftwaffe* began the campaign against the Soviet Union totally convinced of its superiority in both men and machines. However, this assumption proved to be as false in the air as it was on the ground. Among the designers who provided the Soviet air force with some very capable fighters was Aleksandr S. Yakovlev, whose previous design activities had been confined to gliders and sporting aircraft. His first fighter, the Yakovlev Yak-1, first

RIGHT: *The personal aircraft of Major-General Zakharov, commanding 303rd Fighter Aviation Division in 1944. It carries* the Order of the Red Banner on the engine cowling and his personal emblem below the cockpit.

BELOW: *Allowed to choose any fighter, the French-manned Normandie-Niemen Group selected the excellent Yak-3.*

flew in March 1939 and entered service in July 1941, proving an immediate success. Development could not stand still and an improved version, the Yak-1M, quickly led to the Yak-3. At the time a more powerful engine was not available, so extra performance was obtained by reducing the overall size of the airframe, which resulted in lower weight and reduced drag. The prominent under-nose oil cooler was replaced by two smaller, wing-root coolers and the rear fuselage was cut-down and a new, simple, two-piece canopy provided all-round vision. As a final touch, the entire exterior was given a thick coat of hard-wearing wax polish and all these measures combined to increase maximum speed from 373mph (600km/h) to 404mph (650km/h). One area where no improvement was made, however, was in armament, where the Yak-3's single

20mm cannon and two 12.7mm machine guns compared rather unfavourably with the Bf 109G-6's single 30mm cannon, two 13mm machine guns over the engine and a further two machine guns under the wings.

The more powerful VK-107 engine became available and this was fitted to the Yak-3 airframe. Tests showed it to have a maximum speed some 60–70mph (96–113km/h) faster than either the Bf 109 or Fw 190, but this re-engined aircraft was too late to see combat service in World War II.

BELOW: *The Yak-3's performance was a great shock to* Luftwaffe *pilots. On one occasion 18 Yak-3s met 30 German fighters and shot down 15 for the loss of one of their own.*

BELOW RIGHT: *An early production Yak-3. Later versions had the Klimov VK-107 engine, while trials were conducted with two ramjets and even a tail-mounted liquid-fuel rocket which gave a truly dramatic rate of climb.*

EASTERN FRONT: 1943–1945.

The Yak-3 first flew operationally during the Battle of Kursk in the summer of 1943 and it was so successful that the *Luftwaffe* recognised that the days of superiority were over. Indeed, in early 1944 a *Luftwaffe* order was issued instructing pilots to "avoid combat below 5,000m (16,000ft) with Yakovlev fighters lacking an oil cooler under the nose" (ie, Yak-3). To show what Yak-3s could do when properly handled, in an engagement on 14 July 1944 a force of 18 met 30 *Luftwaffe* fighters and destroyed 15 of them for the loss of one of its own number. The Normandie-Nieman Group was fighting on the Eastern Front and the French volunteers were so respected by the Soviets that they were offered the choice of any British, American or Soviet fighter they cared to name. They unhesitatingly chose the Yak-3 and went on to score the last 99 of their 273 victories on this excellent machine.

AVRO LANCASTER

SPECIFICATIONS

COUNTRY OF ORIGIN: Great Britain.

TYPE: high- and low-altitude strategic bomber.

MANUFACTURER: A.V. Roe Limited.

WEIGHTS: empty 36,900lb (16,705kg); normal loaded 68,000lb (30,800kg); overload with 22,000lb (9,980kg) bomb 70,000lb (31,750kg).

DIMENSIONS: span 102.0ft (31.1m); length 69.3ft (21.1m); height 19.6ft (6.0m).

ENGINES: all except Mark II – 4 x Rolls-Royce or Packard Merlin 20 or 22, vee-12, liquid-cooled, each 1,650hp; Mark II only – 4 x Bristol Hercules VI, 14-cylinder two-row radials, each 1,650hp.

PERFORMANCE: max speed 287mph (462km/h) at 11,500ft (3,500m); cruising speed 210mph (338km/h); climb at max weight to 20,000ft (6,095m) 41 minutes; service ceiling 24,500ft (7,467m); range with 14,0000lb (6,350kg) bombs 1,660 miles (2,675km).

WEAPONS: all – nose and dorsal turrets with two 0.303in Browning; tail turret with 4 x 0.303in Browning; Mark II – additional ventral turret with two 0.303in Brownings; internal normal bomb load 14,000lb (6,350kg); internal maximum 22,000lb (9,979kg) "Earthquake" bomb.

CREW: seven.

DESIGN HISTORY

The Avro Lancaster evolved from the Avro Manchester, which was powered by two Rolls-Royce 24-cylinder Vulture engines and suffered from a host of problems, including poor performance and unreliable engines. It was then decided to retain the fuselage and tail (albeit with some modifications) and to fit a longer-span wing, mounting four Rolls-Royce Merlin engines. The first of these flew in early 1941 and was an instant success, being placed into immediate production; deliveries began in early 1942, followed by the first operation on 17 April 1942.

Total production, including in Canada, was 7,377, of which 3,425 were Mark I (Rolls-Royce Merlin), 300 were Mark II (Bristol Hercules) and 3,039 Mark III (Rolls-Royce/Packard Merlin). Other variants included the Mark I (Special) which could carry two 12,000lb (5,443kg) "Tallboy" bombs or a single 22,000lb (9,979kg) "Earthquake" bomb, the

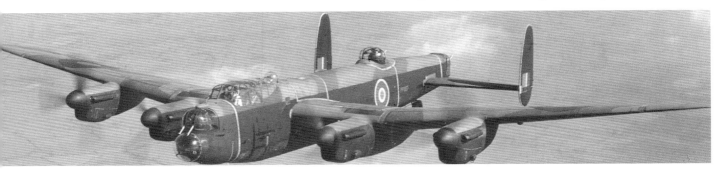

ABOVE: *The splendid Avro Lancaster was the right aircraft at the right time. Together with the other great British heavy bomber, the Handley-Page Halifax, it provided the "punch" required by Bomber Command in providing the British share of the Allied bomber attack.*

LEFT: *The normal payload for a Lancaster was up to 14,000lb (6,350kg) of bombs, although by the war's end a single 22,000lb (9,979kg) "Earthquake" bomb could be carried, instead. With special modifications one of Barnes Wallis's dam-busting bombs could also be delivered.*

ABOVE: *A Lancaster is silhouetted by the fire and flak in this shot taken from a higher flying Lancaster over Hamburg. This target was regularly bombed by both British and Americans and the city centre and the port area were totally devastated by the bombing attacks.*

LEFT: *One alternative to high-explosive bombs were incendiaries, such as this load being dropped on the German city of Duisberg, during a daylight raid in 1944. Duisberg was in the Ruhr, another area regularly targeted by the British RAF's Bomber Command.*

unarmed Mark VI with high-altitude Merlins and four-bladed propellers, and the Dambusters version with cut-away bomb doors and a special device for spinning-up the drum-shaped skipping bombs designed by Dr Barnes Wallis.

The Lancaster had an all-metal fuselage constructed from five pre-assembled sections; the wings also consisted of five sections. Virtually half the 69.3ft (21.1m) length was taken up by the massive 33ft 10(m) long bomb-bay.

ATTACK ON M.A.N. FACTORY, AUGSBURG: 17 APRIL 1942.

The Lancaster's first operation was by four aircraft from the first Lancaster unit – No 44 (Rhodesia) Squadron – in a "gardening" (ie, mining) attack in the Heligoland Bight on 3 March 1940. The next week two Lancasters, each carrying 5,040lb (2,286kg) of incendiaries flew on their first bombing operation against Essen.

Nos 44 and 97 Squadrons carried out an epic attack on the M.A.N factory at Augsburg, in southern Germany, where half the diesel engines for Germany's U-boat fleet were manufactured. The raid was preceded by three practice flights, starting over Selsey Bill on the south coast of England and taking them at very low-level north over Lanark on the Scottish border to the simulated target at Inverness, following which the Lancasters flew back to their bases in Lincolnshire, in eastern England.

The raid was carried out on 17 April 1942 by 12 unescorted Lancaster Is, six from each squadron, with Squadron-Leader Nettleton (44 Squadron) in command. There were several diversionary operations, but a formation of some 25-30 Bf 109s found the low-flying Lancasters over France and in a series of attacks managed to shoot down four. The remaining eight carried on, of which four, badly damaged were forced to turn back. Nettleton and one other Lancaster reached the target where they dropped their delayed-action bombs despite intense anti-aircraft fire, although this then felled the second aircraft. Nettleton managed to nurse his damaged aircraft back to base. He was awarded the Victoria Cross, the first of 10 such awards to Lancaster crews.

Lancasters took part in a number of epic operations, including the Dam Busters raid (16 May 1943) and the sinking of the battleship *Tirpitz* (12 November 1944). Like the USAAF B-17s and B-24s and RAF Halifaxes, however, their real strength lay in the day-by-day, sustained pounding of the Third Reich, which proved to the German population as a whole that their leaders could not protect them. During the air war in North-West Europe Lancaster bombers made 156,190 individual sorties of which 148,403 were bombing raids, an invaluable contribution to the final victory.

LEFT: *Lancaster bombers, seen here "somewhere over Germany", made 148,403 individual bombing sorties over Western Europe, a vital element of the Allied strategic plan for the RAF and USAAF to bring Germany to its knees.*

ABOVE: *44 Squadron Lancaster I L7578 with identical national and squadron markings to those used by aircraft taking part in the Augsburg raid on 17 April 1942. The fuselage roundel was later reduced in brightness and size.*

BELOW: *A flight of Avro Lancasters of 207 Squadron RAF flies peacefully over the English countryside. The first Lancaster operation took place on 17 April 1942 and a grand total of 7,377 of all types were built in factories in Britain and Canada.*

DE HAVILLAND DH 98 MOSQUITO B.IV

SPECIFICATIONS

COUNTRY OF ORIGIN: Great Britain.
TYPE: high-speed day bomber.
MANUFACTURER: de Havilland Aircraft Company.
WEIGHTS: empty 14,100lb (6,696kg); normal loaded 22,500lb (10,206kg) .
DIMENSIONS: span 54.2ft (16.5m); length 40.8ft (12.4m); height 15.3ft (4.7m).
ENGINES: 2 x Rolls-Royce Merlin 21 vee-12, liquid-cooled; each 1,230hp.
PERFORMANCE: max speed 380mph (612km/h); initial climb 1,870ft/min (570m/min); service ceiling 34,500ft (10,520m); range 1,860 miles (2,990km).
WEAPONS: normal bomb load internal four 500lb (227kg) bombs; some with bulged bomb bay for one 2,000lb (1,814kg) bomb.
CREW: two.

DESIGN HISTORY

De Havilland planned the Mosquito in October 1938 as a high-speed, unarmed daylight bomber, which would be made of wood to ease the strain on strategic materials during the war which was clearly coming. The.Air Ministry showed no interest, however, suggesting instead that the company should make wings for existing heavy bomber designs, in metal. It was not until 1940 that the Air Ministry agreed, with great reluctance, to allow the firm to produce a prototype, although it was considered that the only possible role for such an unarmed aircraft would be reconnaissance. The first prototype was built in great secrecy and flew on 25 November 1940; it was an instant success and official reluctance was transformed into an almost embarrassing enthusiasm. Production orders were immediately placed and when the run ended some 7,781 had been manufactured in a wide variety of marks, in factories in Australia, Britain and Canada.

The first operational mission was carried out by a Mk1 photo-recce machine which flew over German naval bases at Brest, La Pallice and Bordeaux in France on 21 September 1941, following which Mk II fighters became operational in May 1942, armed with four 0.303in machine guns in a solid nose, with four 20mm cannon below them in the forward bomb-bay. The first bomber version, Mark IV Series I, did not enter service, but the Mk IV Series II entered service in April 1942 which had the unprecedented speed for a bomber of 382mph (611km/h) at 22,000ft (6,705m). A grand total of 43 different marks were built, covering roles such as night fighter, fighter-bomber, intruder, ground-attack, torpedo strike, shipping strike and trainer, as well as increasingly capable photo-reconnaissance aircraft, bombers and fighters; there was even a carrier-borne version (Mark XXX) with power-folding wings and an arrester hook.

LEFT: *The Mosquito design proved extremely versatile, with many variants produced for a variety of roles. This is an RAF Coastal Command Mk XVIII fighter.*

TOP RIGHT: *Testimony to the accuracy of 21 and 464 Squadrons' attack on Amiens prison. Of 700 prisoners, 102 were killed, but 258 escaped.*

RIGHT: *Among the missions undertaken by Mosquitoes were high-speed, low-level, precision attacks. Here a Mosquito B IV of 105 Squadron RAF is prepared for such an operation.*

ATTACK ON AMIENS PRISON: 18 FEBRUARY 1944.

A wide variety of Mosquito types took part in many operations from 1942 onwards, but one of the most spectacular uses of the aircraft was in very precise, fast and very low-level attacks. One of the first was by two separate flights of three Mosquitoes which attacked Berlin in broad daylight on 30 January 1943. The first attack came in the morning just as *Luftwaffe* commander, Hermann Goering, was about to address a large rally, and the second in mid-afternoon as the Propaganda Minister, Josef Goebbels, was starting his address to a second rally. One aircraft was lost and not a great deal of damage was done, but both meetings were very publicly disrupted and the message was very clear – despite all their proud boats the Nazi leaders could not guarantee the safety of Germans, even in their capital city.

Another precision attack was against Amiens prison, northern France, on 18 February 1944, where over a hundred French Resistance men were due to be executed by the Gestapo. Eighteen FB MK VIs attacked, blowing holes in both the prison walls, in the prison itself, and in the guards' accommodation block. There were some 700 prisoners in the jail of whom 102 were killed, but 258 escaped, while the raid commander, Group-Captain Pickard was shot down and killed in the return flight. The next precision raid (31 October 1944) was by 24 Mosquitoes in a 1,235-mile (1,988km) round trip against the Gestapo headquarters in Aarhus, Denmark. The building was destroyed together with the papers and documents which were being used by the Gestapo in its campaign against the Danish Resistance.

After initial derision at a modern aircraft made of plywood, the Mosquito came to be known as the "Wooden Wonder" and made a substantial contribution to winning the war.

SPECIFICATIONS

COUNTRY OF ORIGIN: Great Britain.

TYPE: three-seat carrier-borne torpedo-bomber.

MANUFACTURER: Fairey Aviation.

IN SERVICE: 1936–1945.

WEIGHTS: empty 4,700lb (2,132kg); max loaded 9,250lb (4,1956kg).

DIMENSIONS: span 45.5ft (13.9m); length 36.3ft (11.1m); height 12.8ft (3.9m).

ENGINE: 1 x Bristol Pegasus IIIM3 9-cylinder radial air-cooled supercharged; 770hp at 2,200rpm at sea-level.

PERFORMANCE: max speed 132mph (212km/h) at sea level; economical cruise 104mph (167km/h) at 5,000ft (1,525m); initial climb 560ft/min (171m/min); time to 5,000ft (1,525m) at max weight 10 minutes; range at economical cruise with 1,500lb (680kg) weapon load, 546 miles (878km).

WEAPONS: 1 x Vickers 0.303in MG (forward-firing, fixed); 1 x Lewis 0.303in (flexible mount, rear cockpit); 1 x 18in (457mm) Mk XIIB torpedo (1,610lb/730kg) or one Mine "A" (1,500lb/680kg); or 1,500lb (680kg) bombs.

FAIREY SWORDFISH MK I

DESIGN HISTORY

The Fairey Swordfish was an anachronism, even when it entered service in summer 1936, being a biplane with a low-powered radial engine, with a theoretical cruising speed of 104mph (167km/h) but considerably less in a head-wind. It had a crew of three (pilot, observer and telegraphist/air gunner) and could be armed with either a single torpedo or mine, or bombs. What it lacked in speed the Swordfish made up for in docility, being exceptionally easy to fly. It was very slow and able to turn inside any modern, high-speed fighter, and when attacked by Bf 109s and Fw 190s during the "Channel Dash" in 1942, the German fighters had to lower their flaps and undercarriages to reduce their speed to the point where they could attack such a

OPERATION JUDGEMENT – BRITISH ATTACK ON TARANTO: 12 NOVEMBER 1940.

The British Mediterranean Fleet attacked the Italian Fleet on the night of 11/12 November 1940, the British force comprising the carrier *Illustrious,* escorted by four cruisers and four destroyers. The primary targets, lying in the harbour of Taranto, were six battleships, four of which (*Duilio, Giulio Cesare, Doria, Cavour*) were launched in 1911–1913, but thoroughly refitted and modernised in the 1930s, while the other two (*Littorio, Vittorio Veneto*) were brand-new.

The first attack wave, launched just before 2100 comprised 12.Swordfish; six with torpedoes, four with bombs and two with

a mixture of bombs and flares, and all carrying extra fuel tanks. On leaving *Illustrious* the formation became split up in cloud, losing four aircraft, but the remaining eight pressed on. Taranto was defended by 21 anti-aircraft batteries and 200 machine guns, supported by many searchlights, with two lines of barrage balloons and several torpedo net arrays in the outer harbour. Despite lacking radar, the Italians detected the approaching aircraft and the defences were ready as the attack commenced.

The two flare-carrying aircraft swung off to drop their flares behind the target, silhouetting the ships for the torpedo bombers as these approached in line-ahead at their attack height of 30ft (9m), jinking through the barrage balloon cables and then skimming across the mole. All three aircraft aimed their torpedoes at the *Cavour,* scoring three hits; the leader was shot down immediately after releasing his torpedo (he and his observer were saved), but the other two aircraft survived.

One torpedo-bomber that had been lost in the clouds now caught up and attacked *Littorio,* scoring a hit, while a fifth Swordfish approached *Littorio* from the north and also scored a hit. The remaining aircraft of the first wave also approached from the north; it attacked *Vittorio Veneto,* but the torpedo malfunctioned. The second wave approached from the north-west and the first two attacked *Littorio,* the third *Duilio* and the fourth *Vittorio Veneto,* although the latter's torpedo malfunctioned. The fifth aircraft was hit and blown up as it started its attack run, killing both its crew.

Littorio (three hits) and *Duilio* (one hit) were out of action for many months, while *Cavour* (one hit) was sunk, and although salvaged never returned to service. Damage was also scored against other ships in the harbour and shore targets. This attack at Taranto was undoubtedly the Swordfish's finest hour, although it also achieved a remarkable record in attacking enemy surface ships (for example, *Bismarck*) and U-boats. Nevertheless, it is no reflection on the gallantry of its crews to suggest that they could have been better served by a more modern and sophisticated aircraft.

slow-moving aircraft. There was, however, a major weakness in that in a torpedo attack the Swordfish was required to make a steady approach run at constant height (50ft/15m) and speed (90kt/137km/h) during which time it was exceptionally vulnerable.

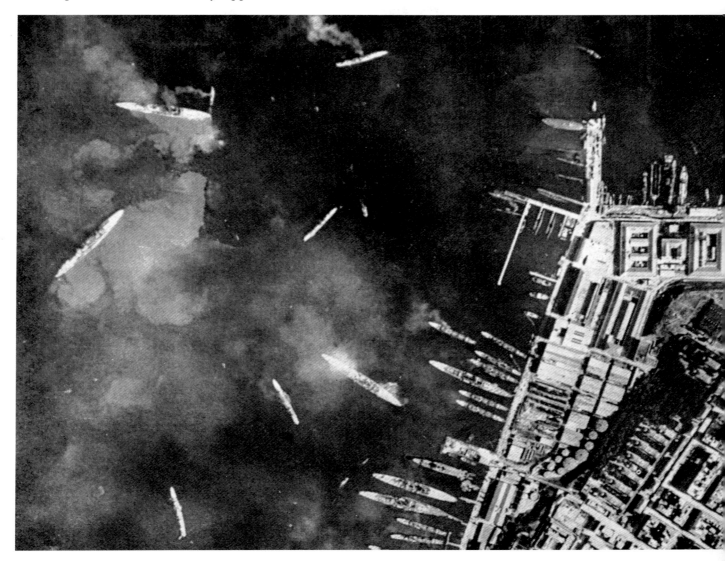

ABOVE: *Taranto inner harbour on the day after the attack. Two damaged cruisers (top left) leak oil and one is still on fire. The battleships were in the outer harbour.*

LEFT: *A Swordfish about to take off from HMS* Illustrious, *whose radio masts have been lowered.*

RIGHT: *Swordfish aboard HMS* Ark Royal *in the Mediterranean in 1941. The Swordfish was an anachronism, even as it entered service, but achieved some remarkable successes.*

HAWKER HURRICANE I

SPECIFICATIONS

COUNTRY OF ORIGIN: Great Britain.
TYPE: single-seat fighter.
MANUFACTURER: Hawker Aircraft Ltd.
IN SERVICE: 1939–1945.
WEIGHTS: empty 4,670lb (2,118g); loaded 6,600lb (2,994kg).
DIMENSIONS: span 40.0ft (12.2m); length 32.0ft (9.8m); height 13.0ft (4.0m).
ENGINE: 1 x Rolls-Royce Merlin III, vee-12, liquid-cooled (with variable-pitch, three-bladed propeller).
PERFORMANCE: max speed 318mph (511km/h); initial climb 2,520ft/min (768m/min); service ceiling 36,000ft (11,000.m); range about 460 miles (740km).
WEAPONS: 8 x 0.303in Browning machine guns in wing (each 333 rounds).

DESIGN HISTORY

Hawker's chief designer, Sydney Camm, started work in 1934,on a monoplane conversion of the Fury biplane, with a Goshawk engine, fixed undercarriage and four wing-mounted machine guns. This was, however, altered on the drawing-board to incorporate the latest developments, including the new Rolls-Royce PV.12 engine (later named the "Merlin"), an inwards-retracting undercarriage and the unheard-of armament of eight wing-mounted machine guns. The Air

BELOW: *Hawker Hurricane Mk I of No 73 Squadron RAF, in 1939/40. This was one of a batch of 500 built by Gloster.*

BELOW: *Three Hurricanes over France in 1939/40. They are flying in the RAF's rigidly enforced "vic" (V) formation, developed in peace and used throughout the Battle of Britain and well into 1941, before it was discarded in the light of battle experience.*

Ministry wrote Specification F.36/37 around this new fighter and, following tests with the prototype, which flew for the first time on 6 November 1935, placed an immediate order for 600.

The first Hurricane squadron became operational in February 1938 and during the production run of the Hurricane I a number of major improvements were incorporated. These included replacing the original fabric-covered wings with metal-skinned wings, and the original two-bladed fixed-pitch propeller Merlin II with the more powerful Merlin III with a three-bladed, variable pitch (later constant-speed) propeller. Other improvements included an armoured bulkhead in front of the cockpit and a bullet-proof windscreen. The cannon-armed Hurricane II entered service just too late to play a part in the Battle of Britain.

ABOVE: *"Scramble!" Pilots run for their Hurricanes as ground crew start engines and others stand by to help them don their parachutes before entering the cockpit.*

LEFT CENTRE: *Five Hurricanes scramble from a desert airstrip. Apart from the Battle of Britain, Hurricanes also proved successful in the early stages of the North African campaign as an interceptor and later as a tank-buster armed with twin underwing 40mm cannon.*

RIGHT: *Royal Auxiliary Air Force (RAuxAF) squadrons made an invaluable contribution to the battle. Here two Hurricanes of 501 Squadron RAuxAF scramble from Gravesend airfield on 15 August 1940.*

ABOVE: *"Cruising" formation, showing three sections, the photograph being taken from the lead aircraft of the fourth section. RAF tactical formations were very rigid.*

LEFT: *Squadron Leader "Ginger" Lacey, the highest scoring "ace" in the Battle of Britain, who shot down five enemy aircraft in France and a further 18 during the Battle of Britain in 1940.*

RIGHT: *The pilots of 242 Squadron at Duxford in 1940 with their famous CO, Douglas Bader (fourth from right). At least four of the ten in this picture were killed during the war.*

BATTLE OF BRITAIN: 10 JULY–31 OCTOBER 1940

At the beginning of the Battle of Britain there were 2,309 Hurricane Is in service (compared to 1,383 Spitfires) and the type equipped 32 squadrons. It was found to be an ideal bomber destroyer, could out-turn any other monoplane fighter, and was much stronger and able to withstand more battle-damage than the German Bf 109, although its all-round performance was not as good and if a Bf 109 pilot decided to use speed to disengage, a Hurricane pilot could not catch him.

One Hurricane pilot, Sergeant "Ginger" Lacey, was the highest scoring British pilot in the Battle of Britain. Lacey went to France with 501 Squadron in May 1940 where he shot down two fighters (one Bf 109, one Bf 110) and three bombers (He 111) before returning to England on 18 June. On 20 July he shot down a Bf 109, but his score increased rapidly in August with five confirmed kills: two dive-bombers (Ju 87), one bomber (Ju 88) and two fighters (Bf 109s). He also damaged another five: one dive-bomber (Ju 87); two bombers (one Do 17, one Do 215) and two fighters (one Bf 109, one Bf 110). In the first week of September he shot down two fighters (Bf 109s) in the same fight and then went on leave.

He returned to duty on then 13th by which time his squadron had moved to Kenley, south of London, where he

became involved in a most remarkable episode. It started when his squadron received a telephone call stating that a lone enemy bomber was over London, but that since the entire south-east was under dense cloud the fighter controllers would be able to use radar to guide the pilot to the target but that he would almost certainly then have to bale out. Therefore the mission would only be flown by a volunteer and Lacey immediately stepped forward.

Following take-off, Lacey broke cloud at 14,000ft (4,270m) and after a long stalk under ground direction he spotted the bomber (it was an Heinkel He 111) and dived on it, killing the upper gunner. He then followed the Heinkel through the next cloud bank and when both aircraft emerged he found that the dead gunner had been removed and a new man fired, damaging Lacey's Hurricane and setting it on fire. Lacey fired off all his ammunition at the Heinkel and then baled out, but as he dropped to the ground he saw the Heinkel crash. He was back with his squadron that night. Two days later Lacey flew no less than four sorties, during which he shot down three enemy aircraft and severely damaged a fourth.

The Hurricane's achievements in the Battle of Britain have been overshadowed by those of the Spitfire, but they were just as great, especially in the hands of pilots such as Lacey.

SUPERMARINE SPITFIRE IA

SPECIFICATIONS

COUNTRY OF ORIGIN: Great Britain.

TYPE: single-seat fighter.

MANUFACTURER: Supermarine Aviation Works (Vickers), Southampton.

IN SERVICE: 1939–1945.

WEIGHTS: empty 4,517lb (2,049g); loaded 5,844lb (2,651kg).

DIMENSIONS: span 36.8ft (11.2m); length 29.9ft (9.1m); height 11.4ft (3.5m).

ENGINE: 1 x Rolls-Royce Merlin III, vee-12, liquid-cooled (with de Havilland Hamilton two-pitch, three-bladed propeller).

PERFORMANCE: max speed 346mph (557km/h); cruise 304mph (489km/h) at 15,000ft (4,570m); initial climb 2,530ft/min (700m/min); time to 15,000ft 6.85 minutes; service ceiling 30,500ft (9,300m); range about 415 miles (668km).

WEAPONS: 8 x 0.303in Browning machine guns in wing (each 300 rounds).

DESIGN HISTORY

Among the most famous aircraft in aviation history, the Spitfire was designed by R. J. Mitchell to Specification F.37/34, using the new Rolls-Royce PV.12 engine, which was later named the Merlin. The Spitfire was the first all-metal, stressed skin aircraft to go into production in Britain, the first production version, Spitfire I, being powered by the 1,030hp Merlin II driving a two-blade, fixed-pitch wooden propeller, and armed with four wing-mounted Browning machine guns. This entered service in 1938.

Naturally, development was rapid, the major one being the replacement of the Merlin by the more powerful version Merlin III and a new three-bladed propeller, with two-stage pitch, which did not

BELOW: *This Mk IIA, the gift of members of the Observer Corps, was flown by Squadron Leader Don Finlay, commanding officer of 41 Squadron in 1940.*

improve maximum speed but did greatly improve the climb. The armament was also increased to eight Brownings. The first production versions had a flat-roofed canopy but many pilots said that they banged their heads on this, so a new bulged roof was fitted, which became a characteristic of the Spitfire profile. These changes, incorporated from the 78th production machine onwards, led to a change in designation to Spitfire IA, which was the type in service at the time of the Battle of Britain.

ABOVE: *Supermarine Spitfires of 610 Squadron in the "search-and-cruise" formation. They still fly in threes, but the distances between the "vics" have been considerably increased as a result of battle experience.*

LEFT: *Groundcrew help a 19 Squadron Spitfire Mk IA returning to Duxford after a Battle of Britain mission. The narrow track undercarriage was one of the few negative features of the design.*

RIGHT: *The Spitfire's elegant lines earned it a special place in British affections, although it proved a difficult aircraft to manufacture, especially the wing leading edges.*

ABOVE: *The Spitfire remained in front-line service throughout the war. This example is wearing "invasion stripes" and is being rearmed in a temporary base in a French wheatfield field in July 1944.*

LEFT: *The Spitfire achieved a more glamorous image than the Hurricane, but in fact it only represented one-third of Fighter Command's strength during the Battle of Britain and gained one-third of the total victories over the Luftwaffe.*

ABOVE RIGHT: *A view no enemy would like to see as Spitfires of 610 (County of Chester) Squadron, RAuxAF close in on the camera. Air and groundcrews of the RAuxAF fought with great distinction alongside the regular RAF men during the Battle of Britain.*

BATTLE OF BRITAIN: 10 JULY–31 OCTOBER 1940.

The Battle of Britain lasted from 10 July to 31 October 1940, a period of 82 days. Phase I consisted of *Luftwaffe* probes intended to test and weaken British defences, with attacks on coastal convoys coupled with massive fighter sweeps over southern England. Phase II, which started in the second week in August was intended to destroy RAF Fighter Command as an effective force and consisted of heavy attacks on airfields and radar stations in southern England. Without having achieved total success the German attack then switched on 7 September to Phase III which had a two-fold aim: to cow the civil population and to force the British fighters into the air where they would be destroyed. This included Sunday 15 September, now marked as "Battle of Britain Day", when 56 German aircraft were shot down and 12 force-landed against British losses of 27 (post-war figures in both cases). Even more important than the simple figures, however, was the effect on morale on both sides: the British felt that they had been victorious, while the Germans considered that they were outnumbered and beset by problems. Major daylight attacks on London continued until the end of September, when attacks switched to night bombing, adding to those already being undertaken against Liverpool and Coventry. Then came Phase IV, which lasted from late

September until the end of October, with yet heavier night bombing, accompanied by a few daylight fighter and fighter-bomber sweeps by the *Luftwaffe* in daylight.

During the course of the Battle of Britain, the *Luftwaffe* lost 1,792 aircraft, of which 610 were Bf 109s, while the British lost 1,172 aircraft, of which 403 were Spitfires (Hurricanes – 631). However, by the end the rate of RAF losses was falling while that of the Germans was climbing. Also, RAF aircrew who bailed out or crash-landed generally did so over friendly territory and returned to the fight, while German aircrew either landed on British territory or in the Channel and were usually captured.

As a result of the Battle of Britain, the Spitfire won an international reputation, much of which was thoroughly deserved. It was not, however, without its drawbacks, being not quite as fast on the level as the Bf 109, while its float carburettor limited certain manoeuvres so that a German fighter in trouble could half-roll and dive, a manoeuvre not open to the Spitfire. Also, its rifle-calibre machine guns did not have the same "punch" or range as the Bf 109's cannon, although the eight machine guns were devastating if the pilot could get close enough. Nevertheless, its own pilots had supreme faith in the Spitfire and its enemies learned to treat it with great respect.

BOEING B-17G FORTRESS

COUNTRY OF ORIGIN: United States of America.

TYPE: high altitude strategic bomber.

MANUFACTURER: Boeing Airplane Company, Seattle, USA.

IN SERVICE: 1939–1945.

WEIGHTS: empty 32,720lb (14,855kg); max loaded 65,600lb (29,700kg).

DIMENSIONS: span 103.8ft (31.6m); length 74.8ft (22.8m); height 19.0ft (5.8m).

ENGINES: 4 x Wright R-1820-97 Cyclone nine-cylinder radials with turbo-charger; each 1,200hp.

PERFORMANCE: max speed 287mph (462km/h); cruising speed 182mph (293km/h); service ceiling 35,000ft (10,670m); range with max bomb load 1,100 miles (1,760km).

WEAPONS: twin 0.5in Brownings in chin, dorsal, ball and tail turrets; one in each waist position; normal internal bomb load 6,000lb (2,724kg); max internal 12,800lb (5,800kg).

CREW: six to ten.

DESIGN HISTORY

When it first flew in 1935, the XB-17 was the most advanced bomber in the world, with four Pratt & Whitney Hornet engines, retracting undercarriage, eight-man crew and stowage for eight 600lb (272kg) bombs. Thirteen Y1B-17 test machines were built, all with Wright Cyclone engines, but the first production version, B-17B, had revised nose, rudder and flaps, while the B-17C had additional weapons, armour and self-sealing tanks. The major production models were the B-17E, with a totally redesigned tail incorporating a rear turret, followed by the B-17F (3,405 built) and the B-17G (8,680 built), the last having the definitive chin turret and flush staggered waist guns.

BELOW: *Boeing B-17G-25 serving with 96th Bomb Group at Snetterton Heath, UK, in 1944. The heavy armament comprised twin 0.5in MGs in the chin, dorsal, ball and tail turrets, and single MGs either side of the nose, above the radio compartment and on each side of the waist.*

ABOVE: Forward armament of this late model B-17G comprised two 0.50in MGs in the Bendix chin turret and two 0.5in MGs in the dorsal turret. In addition, there were was one 0.5in MG each side of the nose, which was fired from behind a fixed screen.

LEFT: The "combat box" formation was developed to provide mutual protection between a large number of aircraft, but it took several hours for the full formation gradually to build up to its full size prior to leaving the skies over England.

RIGHT: The definitive model of the B-17 was the "G" of which 8,680 were built. It was a formidable machine, carrying a maximum internal bombload of 12,800lb (5,800kg) and a crew of up to ten men. It was armed with ten 0.5in Browning machine guns.

LEFT: *By 1944 the bombardier with his Norden sight flew in the lead aircraft of a "combat box". All aircraft in the box then dropped their entire bomb loads simultaneously on his order.*

RIGHT: *Pilots 1/Lt Malcolm Brown (left), who looks particularly weary, and Capt George Mackin (right) shake hands on completion of the fiftieth operational mission by their aircraft, B-17F "Knockout Dropper."*

TOP LEFT: *A USAAF B-17 flies over a bombed airfield in Germany, with aircraft burning in the dispersal area.*

ABOVE: *One of the final World War II air attacks on Germany was a combined American/ British attack against Dresden. Here USAAF B-17s carry out a daylight raid on railway yards in the city on 17 April 1945.*

RIGHT: *USAAF bomber formations flew at different heights and this picture shows why lower aircraft were sometimes hit by bombs from friendly aircraft flying above them.*

NORTH-WEST EUROPE: 1942–1945.

Despite the name "Fortress", early B-17s had several vulnerable spots, including ahead, covered by only one machine gun, and abeam below the horizontal, since the dorsal turret could not be depressed sufficiently. The first measure was to resite the weapons to improve their arcs of fire, and the second was to assemble bombers into groups for mutual protection. After various experiments the "combat box" was evolved, consisting of three squadrons, each of six aircraft flying in two "vics" of three, the second slightly lower than the first, while within the box the second squadron flew higher than the first and the third lower. Once such boxes had been perfected, the next stage, reached in 1944, was "wings" of three "combat boxes" (ie, a total of 54 aircraft). These formations enabled the B-17s to offer each other maximum mutual support, although the frontal arc of the leading squadron remained a problem, not least because, when attacked from ahead, closing speed was some 600mph (966km/h). It was then decided that only the leading and one other aircraft would carry bombsights, which were removed from all other aircraft, enabling twin machine guns to be mounted in the nose. This meant that only the leading bombardier used his bombsight (or his deputy if the lead aircraft was lost) and all other aircraft then dropped their bombs on his command. The real solution to bomber defence, however, was the presence of a fighter escort, although they suffered from range limitations until the P-51D Mustang became operational in 1944.

Once airborne, it took some two hours for the B-17s to climb and to sort themselves out into the required formation, which could take as much as two hours, following which they set off in narrow streams. The normal crew was 10 strong (pilot, copilot, navigator, flight engineer, wireless operator, bombardier, belly gunner, two waist gunners and tail gunner) and their B-17G's normal bombload was 4,000lb (1,814kg), either two 2,000lb (907kg) or four 1,000lb (454kg) bombs. The B-17 was very stable, making it a good bombing platform, and also very strong, being capable of absorbing incredible battle damage, with repeated examples of aircraft returning home with large parts of wings, fuselage or tail missing, or with one, two or, in a few cases, three engines unserviceable.

Some 13,000 B-17s were built of which 5,000 lost in action or by accident, the greatest proportion in operations over north-west Europe in 1942/43 – ie, before long-range fighters came into service. Thus, on 17 August 1943, for example, 376 B-17s set out to attack German factories in Schweinfurt, Regensburg and Wiener Neustadt, and, of those, 60 were lost. Schweinfurt alone was attacked again on 14 October 1943, this time by 291 B-17s, with 60 lost, 17 written-off in crashes on their return, and 121 requiring major repairs. Worse than the loss of aircraft, however, was the loss of 648 aircrew killed, wounded and missing. With bombers of the British Royal Air Force and the B-24 Liberators of the USAAF, the B-17 made a war-winning contribution to the bombing attack on Nazi Germany.

BOEING B-29
SUPERFORTRESS

SPECIFICATIONS

COUNTRY OF ORIGIN: United States of America.
TYPE: high altitude strategic bomber.
MANUFACTURER: Boeing Airplane Company.
IN SERVICE: 1944- 1945.
WEIGHTS: empty 74,500lb (33,795kg); max loaded 135,000lb (61,240kg).
DIMENSIONS: span 141.3ft (43.1m); length 99.0ft (30.2m); height 27.8ft (8.5m).
ENGINES: 4 x Wright R-3350-23 Duplex Cyclone 18-cylinder radials, each with two exhaust-driven turbochargers; each 2,200hp.
PERFORMANCE: max speed 357mph (575km/h) at 30,000ft (9,144m); cruising speed 290mph (467km/h); climb to 25,000ft (7,620m) in 43min; .
service ceiling 36,000ft (10,973m); range with 10,000lb (4,540kg) bombs 3,250 miles (5,230km).
WEAPONS: four GE twin 0.5in turrets above and below, sighted from nose or three waist sighting stations; Bell tail turret with own gunner, with one 20mm cannon and twin 0.5in MG; internal max 20,000lb (9,072kg) or one atomic bomb.
CREW: four to six.

DESIGN HISTORY

The development and mass production of the B-29 (Boeing Model 345) was one of the biggest tasks in the history of aviation, and began in 1938 with a study for a four-engined bomber with unprecedented range and payload, using a pressurised cabin, tricycle undercarriage and many other innovations. In January 1942 the USAAF ordered 14 YB-29s and 500 production aircraft "off-the-drawing-board," eight months before the prototype's first flight.

The B-29 set new standards in engine power, gross weight, wing loading, pressurisation, armament, airborne systems and structure. The basic design had a fuselage of circular section, with two pressurised cabins, one occupying the nose, the other a section aft of the wing for the gunners, the two cabins being linked by a tube just large enough for a crewman to crawl through. The tail gunner had his own pressurised compartment. There were two

ABOVE: *The Boeing B-29 was, unquestionably, the finest bomber of World War II, its payload, range, speed and defensive capability all being in a class of their own. Its efforts were concentrated in conventional raids against Japan.*

RIGHT: *The damage wrought by one B-29 on Hiroshima with one atomic bomb was horrifying, although greater damage and many more deaths were actually inflicted on Tokyo in conventional attacks.*

vast bomb bays, one each side of the wing centre section. The wing was stronger than any previously built, and its loading, fantastic by earlier standards, was made possible by enormous, electrically actuated Fowler flaps. The giant engine nacelles, made by Fisher, carried a turbocharger on each side and the engines drove large, four-bladed propellers.

Engineering was a challenge, but so, too, was production, which eventually involved Boeing, Bell, North American, Fisher (General Motors) and Martin, and when production ended in March 1946 more than 3,000 had been produced.

DROPPING THE ATOMIC BOMB: 6/9 AUGUST 1945.

The first B-29 combat mission was flown on 5 June 1944 when 112 aircraft from bases in India attacked Japanese targets around Bangkok, Thailand, a round trip of 2,681 miles (4,300km). By 1945 20 groups based in the Marianas were sending up to 500 B-29s at a time to flatten and burn Japanese cities, and between June and August 1945 there were 60 such raids, concentrated on the 65 cities with a population exceeding 100,000 people. These massive and destructive raids had little visible impact on the Japanese leadership, facing US planners with the alternatives of a massive and undoubtedly costly invasion or the use of the newest and most powerful weapon ever invented: the atomic bomb.

With the United States adopting the latter option, the 509th Composite Group moved to Tinian field in the Marianas in May 1945 and was ready for operations by 1 August. The atomic bombs were brought to the base by ship, the triggers being delivered by the cruiser, USS *Indianapolis*, just before the raid. The first attack involved a single B-29 , piloted by the commanding officer, Colonel Tibbets, and named "Enola Gay" after his mother, carrying a bomb nicknamed "Little Boy". Tibbets took off at 0245 on 6 August with three possible targets and it was not until 0700 that he was told to go to Hiroshima, which he reached at 0815. The bomb was released at a height of 31,600ft (10,000m) and was exploded as an air-burst at 1,900ft (503m) above ground level. This first-ever operational atomic explosion had a yield equivalent to approximately 12–15,000 tons of high-explosive; it killed 78,000 people and wounded another 51,000, while a large area was totally flattened, with 70,000 buildings destroyed and 176,000 people made homeless.

That day President Truman issued a warning to Japan to surrender or face repeated attacks with this new weapon. When he had received no response a second attack was mounted by another B-29, named "Bock's Car" after its captain, which dropped a single "Fat Man" on Nagasaki. This weapon, with a yield equivalent to 22,000 tons of high explosive, killed 50,000 and injured 10,000 more, the lower casualty figure being due to the undulating ground at Nagasaki compared to the flat ground at Hiroshima.

The Japanese surrendered 11 days later and the contribution of these two B-29 bombers to the ending of World War II without the even greater bloodbath that would have been involved in an invasion of Japan is incalculable.

ABOVE: *Colonel Tibbets (centre) with his groundcrew and the aircraft which was named after his wife. He never regretted the raid, which, with that against Nagasaki, prevented an Allied invasion of Japan, which would have claimed many, many more casualties.*

LEFT: *The first atomic bomb dropped on Hiroshima on 5 August 1945 changed the face of warfare for ever – the most significant single raid in aviation history.*

DOUGLAS C-47 SKYTRAIN

SPECIFICATIONS
COUNTRY OF ORIGIN: United States of America.
TYPE: Combat transport.
MANUFACTURER: Douglas Aircraft Company.
IN SERVICE: 1938–1945.
WEIGHTS: empty 16.970lb (7,700kg); loaded 25,200lb (11,432kg); overload limit 33,000lb (14,969kg).
DIMENSIONS: span 95.0ft (29.0m); length 64.5ft (19.6m); height 16.9ft (5.2m).
ENGINES: usually 2 x Pratt & Whitney R-1830-890D or -92 Twin wasp 14-cylinder two-row radials; each 1,200hp.
PERFORMANCE: max speed about 230mph (370km/h); initial climb about 1,200ft/min (366m/min); service ceiling 23,000ft (7,000m); max range 2,125 miles (3,420km).
WEAPONS: none.
CREW: three (pilot, copilot, despatcher/loadmaster).
PAYLOAD: passengers 28-30; paratroops 20; cargo max 7,100lb (3221kg).

DESIGN HISTORY

The most widely used military transport in history, the C-47s origins lay in the 1935 design for the Douglas Sleeper Transport (DST), which was intended principally for commercial North American routes. The design included a modern, all-metal, stressed-skin structure; efficiently cowled engines; wide-span split flaps; retractable main undercarriage; and constant-speed three-bladed propellers. It was an instant success with airlines and a military version was ordered by the United States Army Air Corps, the type entering service as the C-47A in October 1938; most of these had a strengthened cargo floor and large double doors, and many also had cleats for towing gliders.

The C-47B was designed specifically for high-altitude operations was powered by two R-1830-90C engines fitted with two-stage blowers, increasing the ceiling from 23,000ft to 26,000ft (7,000 to 7,925m) to enable them to operate the supply route from India to China over "The Hump". More unusual wartime versions included one with twin-floats, and an engineless glider. The type served with the US Navy as the R4D-5, with the British RAF as the "Dakota", and with many other Allied air forces. When US military production of the C-47 ended in June 1944, some 10,048 of this great aircraft had been produced.

LEFT: *The Douglas DC-3 airliner was taken into military service by the USAAF as the C-47 Skytrain, by the US Navy as the R4D5 and by the British RAF as the Dakota. It provided excellent and reliable service in many operations in all theatres throughout the 1939-45 war.*

BATTLE OF ARNHEM: 17–26 SEPTEMBER 1944

The unglamorous C-47 transport took part in countless missions throughout the war, carrying passengers, paratroops and cargo, and towing gliders, making an immeasurable contribution to the final victory. Operation Market at Arnhem, in Holland, close to the German border, although an British defeat, illustrates just how it operated.

For the Arnhem operation the British airborne forces were allocated 149 US and 130 British C-47s; there were also 494 other aircraft, most of them converted British four-engined bombers. In the first wave of the British assault on 17 September 1944, C-47s of US IX Troop Carrier Command delivered the pathfinder company, which jumped 20 minutes ahead of the main drop to mark the Drop Zones (DZs) some 7 miles (11.3km) from the bridges at Arnhem. The second drop, at H-hour, involved 1st Parachute Brigade, which was carried in its entirety in C-47s. On 18 September C-47s delivered 4th Parachute Brigade, while on 24 September 53 C-47s dropped men of the Polish Parachute Brigade to a DZ south of the river.

Apart from paratroop drops, a considerable part of the air transport effort was devoted to re-supply missions, dropping ammunition, rations and urgently needed supplies, with RAF C-47s playing the major role. Such drops were by no means "milk-runs" and the hazards included attacks by German fighters and AA guns, as well as bad weather, with the condition over English airfields being a particular problem. The final run-in required the aircraft to fly at a constant speed and height, making the aircraft sitting ducks for German AA guns. Of the 163 aircraft taking part in the re-supply operation, 13 were lost. To add to the tragedy, communications problems and the difficulty of seeing ground marker panels from low-flying aircraft meant that, despite the courage of the crews, many resupply drops fell directly into enemy hands.

One of the five Victoria Crosses awarded for the operation was awarded to Flight-Lieutenant Lord, captain of a supply-dropping C-47. On the third day (19 September) his aircraft was hit twice by anti-aircraft fire on the approach. With the starboard engine ablaze Lord descended to the mandatory dropping height of 900ft (274m), holding the aircraft steady as the containers were thrown out. Despite the despatchers' Herculean efforts, two containers remained and Lord, determined to complete his mission, went around for another run. His aircraft, now blazing furiously, crossed the DZ for the second time at 500ft (152m) under constant fire and the two containers were dropped, but when Lord steadied the aircraft for his crew to jump the starboard wing suddenly collapsed and the aircraft crashed. All aboard were killed, except for one who was thrown clear and survived.

LEFT: *Douglas C-47 of 9th Troop Carrier Command drops supplies to US ground troops of 101st Airborne Division cut-off around Bastogne, Belgium, in December 1944 during the "Battle of the Bulge."*

BELOW: *Flying low and straight over drop zones on resupply missions was a hazardous business for the transport crews and* there were many losses. This pilot was fortunate and was able to crash-land his C-47 safely at Bastogne in December 1944.

ABOVE: *An RAF Dakota CIV (C-47B), one of many transports that frequently braved intensive AA fire to para-drop troops and supplies.*

DOUGLAS SBD-5 DAUNTLESS

DESIGN HISTORY

The Northrop BT-1 dive-bomber was designed by the brilliant Ed Heinemann and the first of 54 was delivered in February 1936. This led to much improved Northrop BT-2, but when Northrop was acquired by the Douglas company the aircraft was redesignated SBD-1.

The SBD-1 had a streamlined fuselage and a very broad wing with a horizontal centre-section and sharply tapered outer panels with dihedral. The large perforated split flaps opened fully for use as brakes in steep dive-bombing attacks. The main gear folded inwards into the centre section. The bomb was mounted on a crutch, which swung it forwards and outwards prior to release, to miss the propeller disc, as in the German Ju 87 Stuka. The observer's canopy could be slid forward to enable him to raise his machine guns into the firing position.

Fifty-seven SBD-1s were produced, followed by 87 SBD-2s with greater fuel capacity, 584 SBD-3s with armour and self-sealing tanks, 780 SBD-

SPECIFICATIONS

COUNTRY OF ORIGIN: United States of America.
TYPE: two-seat carrier-borne dive-bomber.
MANUFACTURER: Douglas Aircraft Company.
IN SERVICE: 1940–1945.
WEIGHTS: empty 6,535lb (2,970kg); max loaded 10.700lb (4,8531kg).
DIMENSIONS: span 41.5ft (12.7m); length 33.0ft (10.1m); height 12.9ft (3.9m).
ENGINE: 1 x Wright R-1820-60 9-cylinder, radial; 1,200hp.
PERFORMANCE: max speed 252mph (406km/h); initial climb 1,500ft/min (460m/min); service ceiling 24,300ft (7,430m); range (dive bomber) 456 miles (730km).
WEAPONS: twin 0.5in Browning MG in nose; one (later two) 0.30in Browning MG in rear cockpit. Bomb load one 1,600lb (726kg) on centreline swinging crutch; two 100lb (45kg) bombs, or 250lb (113kg) bombs or depth charges on wing racks.

4s with 24volt electrical system, 3,024 SBD-5s with a 1,200hp engine and 451 SBD-6s with a 1,350hp engine. The US Army Air Corps/Force also took delivery of 953 SBDs of various sub-types, making a grand total of 5,936.

BATTLE OF MIDWAY: 4–6 JUNE 1942.

IJN Admiral Nagumo's attack on the US-held Midway Island in June 1942 was designed to draw the US Pacific Fleet into a trap, but US analysis of Japanese radio traffic revealed his intention and Admiral Nimitz deployed accordingly. The first move was an attack by Midway-based USAAC B-17 bombers, which was followed by a heavy Japanese attack (108 aircraft) on the island, in which 17 US Marine fighters were shot down and seven damaged, although there was little effect on the ground. Next came a US torpedo strike which did no damage. At this point the Japanese aircraft were lined up on their carriers armed with torpedoes for a strike against the US fleet, when Nagumo ordered that they be struck down to the hangars so that the aircraft returning from Midway could land, and that all aircraft were to be armed with bombs for a second strike against Midway.

As the carrier crews sweated to obey the admiral's orders more US strikes came in: first were Marine Corps dive-bombers, followed by B-17 high-level bombers, then Marine bombers, but this strike had little effect. The first US dive-bomber attack was a fiasco, as the aircraft failed to find the Japanese carriers; the SBDs either went on to Midway or returned to their carriers, but 27 Wildcat fighter escorts ran out of fuel and fell into the sea.

Next came 42 Devastator carrier-based torpedo bombers in three waves, but they had no fighter cover and 35 were shot down by Japanese flak and "Zero" fighters. This American strike did no material damage but did force the Japanese carriers to manoeuvre at full speed, breaking their defensive formation, and kept the Japanese combat air patrols engaged at low-level. The chaos aboard the Japanese carriers was worsened by another change-of-mind by Nagumo, who now ordered that the aircraft be rearmed with torpedoes to attack the US fleet.

Thus, when formations of SBD dive-bombers arrived overhead the Japanese carriers' flightdecks were crowded and there was no opposition as the SBDs roared down to attack, causing immense damage. Three carriers, *Akagi*, *Kaga* and *Soryu*, were all hit by bombs and sank that evening, while the fourth carrier, *Hiryu*, was attacked by 34 SBDs at 1700, scoring four hits; it sank at 0900 the next morning.

The SBD Dauntless sank more Japanese shipping than any other Allied weapon, stopped the Imperial Fleet at Midway, played a major role in many other battles and was very popular with its crews, so much so that it outlasted its intended successor, the larger, heavier and far less popular Curtiss SB2C Helldiver.

ABOVE: *SBD-3 on finals aboard the carrier USS* Ranger *in October 1942. The SBD played a crucial role in many battles in the Pacific.*

LEFT: *October 1941 and only two months of peace remain for these Douglas SBD dive-bombers of attack squadron VS-6, their carrier, USS* Enterprise, *and the destroyer/plane guard below.*

RIGHT: *SBDs of VS-6, still in front-line service, are flying to attack Saipan in the Marianas (June 1944). Note bombs under the wings.*

SPECIFICATIONS

COUNTRY OF ORIGIN: United States of America.
TYPE: single-seat naval fighter.
MANUFACTURER: Grumman Aircraft Engineering Corporation.
IN SERVICE: 1943–1945.
WEIGHTS: empty 9,042lb (4,101kg); max loaded 12,186lb (5,5281kg).
DIMENSIONS: span 42.9ft (13.1m); length 33.6ft (10.2m); height 13.0ft (4.0m).
ENGINES: 1 x Pratt & Whitney R-2800-10W Double Wasp 18-cylinder two-row radial; 2,200hp (with water injection).
PERFORMANCE: max speed 376mph (605km/h); initial climb 3,240ft/min (990m/min); service ceiling 37,500ft (11,430m); range (typical) 1,090 miles (1,755km).
WEAPONS: 6 x 0.5in Browning MG in outer wings (400 rounds each). Centre section pylon for 2,000lb (907kg) bomb on centre section pylon; six rockets on underwing attachments.

GRUMMAN F6F-3 HELLCAT

DESIGN HISTORY

The Grumman F6F Hellcat was designed and developed with great speed and then mass-produced at a rate seldom equalled by any other single aircraft factory; following these successes it was then used to such good effect that, from its first day in action, the Allies were winning the air war in the Pacific. Grumman had already produced the F4F Wildcat, which was powered by a Twin Wasp engine (1,050hp) and the XF6F-1 started life as a natural development of the F4F, but powered by the more powerful R-2600 Double Cyclone engine. Within a month of its first flight the even more powerful

ABOVE: *This Grumman F6F Hellcat was in action at Marcus Island on 31 August 1943, just 13 months after the first flight. Note how the huge Double Wasp engine is angled slightly downwards, and the three underwing fuel tanks (only two can be seen).*

RIGHT: *Grumman F6F-3s landing on carrier USS* Enterprise *after attacks on the island of Truk, a major naval base for the IJN, 16 February 1944. Note the complicated wing-folding mechanism and the rearward retracting front undercarriage legs.*

Double Wasp (2,200hp) became available and from the start this aircraft seemed right. As a result, by the autumn of 1942 the production line was at work inside a completely new factory that was actually less complete than the Hellcats inside it! This line flowed at an extraordinary rate, the delivery rates speaking for themselves: 1942–10; 1943 – 2,545; 1944 – 6,139; 1945 – 3,578: a grand total of 12,273, of which 11,000 were produced in two years. These swarms of large, strong and very capable fighters absolutely mastered the Japanese aircraft, and, as a type, the F6F destroyed more than 6,000 hostile aircraft: 4,947 by US Navy carrier squadrons; 209 by land-based Marine Corps squadrons; and the remainder by Allied units.

LEFT: *Grumman F6F-3 Hellcat of US Navy squadron VF-12 about to take off from USS* Enterprise *in a Pacific operation in 1944.*

BELOW: *An F6F-3 pilot is given the latest briefing on the board prior to take off from* Yorktown, *Battle of the Philippine Sea, 19 June 1944.*

BATTLE OF THE PHILIPPINE SEA (FIRST DAY): 19 JUNE 1944.

Perhaps the greatest day in the history of the F6F was 19 June 1944, the first day of the Battle of the Philippine Sea, when Admiral Ozawa, commanding the Japanese fleet, thought (very mistakenly, as it transpired) that he had been offered the opportunity to smash US naval power in the Pacific once and for all by a massive air attack on Vice-Admiral Mitscher's Task Force 58 during the US assault on Saipan.

A Japanese scout aircraft spotted TF.58 late on 18 June and the following morning another scout took over and broadcast plain-language directions for the first attack by radio, which were intercepted and translated on board Mitscher's flagship by a Japanese-speaking officer. As a result, the US fleet knew exactly what was going on and when the first Japanese attack, comprising 64 dive-bombers and torpedo bombers, came in at just after 1000 US fighters were already airborne and waiting for them; they shot down 42 Japanese aircraft at the cost of one minor bomb hit on the battleship *South Dakota*. The same scout unwittingly informed the US fleet of the arrival of the second wave, twice as strong as the first with 128 aircraft, which were

again intercepted as they approached the US fleet. This massive force managed only to achieve a number of near misses and lost an astonishing 97 of their own aircraft downed.

The third wave, 47 strong, came in from a different direction but were again intercepted and lost seven without getting anywhere near the US carriers. The fourth attack, 82 aircraft, arrived just after 1400. Again, they scored no hits on US ships, but lost 54 of their own number shot down, while of the 28 that made it back to their own carriers, 19 were so badly damaged that they were unfit for any further use.

Thus, over the space of some four hours, the Japanese had launched 373 aircraft in four waves. Of these, 242 were shot down, 19 to anti-aircraft fire but the remainder to F6Fs, 50 were shot down in attacks on Guam and 25 or so were lost to other causes. US losses were 23 aircraft. Not surprisingly, the US fliers dubbed this epic air battle the "Great Marianas Turkey Shoot" and the architect of the US victory was the redoubtable F6F, whose mastery over the Japanese was virtually complete.

ABOVE: *An F6F climbs away after launch from the carrier, USS* Monterey *(CVL-26) at the start of the mission against the Japanese island of Okinawa, 10 October 1944. Note also the aircraft being launched from the other carrier and the distant battleship (top left).*

ABOVE: *Hellcats share the deck of the carrier* Enterprise *(CV-6) with Grumman Avengers.*

BELOW LEFT: *A fine portrait of a Grumman F6F-3, an aircraft which proved itself a winner from the start; 12,273 were produced and these destroyed over 6,000 hostile aircraft.*

RIGHT: *An F6F burning on board USS* Lexington *after hitting the crash barrier. The liquid spilling onto the deck is AVGAS, requiring a rapid exit by the pilot, Ensign Ardon R Ives, US Navy.*

LOCKHEED P-38F LIGHTNING

SPECIFICATIONS

COUNTRY OF ORIGIN: United States of America.
TYPE: single-seat fighter.
MANUFACTURER: Lockheed Aircraft Corporation.
IN SERVICE: 1941–1945.
WEIGHTS: empty 12,700lb (5,766kg); loaded 15,500lb (7,030kg).
DIMENSIONS: span 52.0ft (15.9m); length 37.8ft (11.5m); height 12.8ft (3.0m).
ENGINES: 2 x Allison V-1710 49/52 vee-12, liquid-cooled; each 1,325hp.
PERFORMANCE: max speed 391-414mph (630-666km/h); initial climb 2,850ft/min (870m/min); service ceiling 38,000-40,000ft (11,600–12,000m); range at 30,000ft (9,144m) with max fuel 2,260 miles (3,650km).
WEAPONS: one 20mm Hispano cannon, four 0.5in Browning machine guns; 1,000lb (454kg) bombs, torpedoes or fuel tanks on inner wing pylons.

DESIGN HISTORY

The P-38 was designed by Lockheed in response to a 1937 Army Air Corps requirement for a long-range pursuit and escort fighter, with a speed of 360mph (580km/h) at 20,000ft (6,100m), with an endurance at that speed and height of one hour. Lockheed produced a design bristling with innovations, the most eye-catching of which was that it had twin tailbooms, with the pilot seated in a small central nacelle. Power was provided by two Allison engines, which were "handed" (ie, rotated in opposite directions) with GEC turbochargers recessed into the tops of the tailbooms, radiators on the sides of the booms aft of the turbochargers and induction intercoolers in the wing leading edges. The armament was concentrated in the pilot's nacelle and comprised a 23mm cannon and four 0.5in machine guns. To top it all the new aircraft had a tricycle undercarriage, which was rarely fitted in military aircraft at that time. The design posed considerable technical risks, but the prototype flew in January 1939 and the Army Air Corps went ahead with an order, the type entering service in June 1941.

ABOVE: *The P-38 was the Lockheed company's first-ever military design and bristled with innovations, the most striking of which was the twin-boom layout. Note also the turbochargers inset into the tops of the booms and the concentration of weapons in the front of the nacelle. The two Allison engines were "handed" – the propellers rotated in opposite directions, giving zero torque.*

DEATH OF ADMIRAL YAMAMOTO: 18 APRIL 1943.

The P-38 Lightning was involved in one of the most unusual operations in World War II, resulting in the death of Admiral Yamamoto, the great Japanese navy commander. Unites States electronic intelligence units intercepted and decrypted messages concerning Yamamoto's forthcoming morale-boosting visit to the Japanese naval outstations in the Upper Solomon Islands. The decision on whether to take any action was made by US Navy Admiral Nimitz in person, who delegated responsibility for the operation to Admiral Halley. The only aircraft with the required range were the Army Air Force's P-38 Lightnings based at Henderson Field on Guadalcanal and it was decided to attack Yamamoto during his flight from Rabaul to Ballale.

The eighteen P-38s took off at 0525 and followed a very low level route observing strict radio silence. They were almost at their destination when they saw some A6M "Zeroes". Sixteen P-38s climbed to attack the "Zeroes", while the two remaining aircraft zoomed up to 10,000ft (3,000m) before rolling over into the attack on the two G4M "Betty" bombers carrying Yamamoto and his entourage. Despite being under attack from "Zeroes", the two P-38s closed on the G4M "Bettys", shot them down and then climbed to rejoin their comrades for the long flight home.

One P-38 was downed in this operation and six damaged, but the Japanese lost their naval commander-in-chief who was both a revered leader and a brilliant strategist. It was a great success for the P-38 pilots and a victory whose importance was out of all proportion to the numbers involved.

LEFT: *The remains of the Japanese Navy's G4M Betty bomber, which had been carrying Admiral Yamamoto, lie on the jungle floor near Buin on Bougainville island. The Yamamoto attack was a strategic success achieved with minimum risk.*

BOTTOM: *P-38F Lightning (with P-51 and P-47 in background).*

BELOW: *P-38F of 347th Fighter Group, Guadalcanal, February 1943. Production totalled 9,942 for many missions, including PR, bomber, glider tugs, ECM and even as air ambulances.*

NORTH AMERICAN B-25B MITCHELL

SPECIFICATIONS

COUNTRY OF ORIGIN: United States of America.
TYPE: medium bomber.
MANUFACTURER: North American Aviation Inc.
IN SERVICE: 1940–1945.
WEIGHTS: empty 21,100lb (9,580kg); max loaded 26,640lb (12,991kg).
DIMENSIONS: span 67.6ft (20.6m); length 52.9ft (16.1m); height 15.7ft (4.8m).
ENGINES: 2 x Wright R-2600-9 Double Cyclone 14-cylinder, two-row radials; each 1,700hp.
PERFORMANCE: max speed 300mph (483km/h); initial climb 1,500ft/min (460m/min); service ceiling 27,000ft (8,230m); range (typical) 1,500 miles (2,414km).
WEAPONS: twin 0.3in MG in remote-controlled dorsal turret; twin 0.3in MG in retractable ventral turret; bomb load 3,000lb (1,361kg).
CREW: four to six.

DESIGN HISTORY

The B-25 was designed by a company with no previous experience of twin-engined aircraft, bombers, or high-performance military warplanes. It was named after a fearless officer who was court-martialled for his tiresome (to military bureaucrats) advocacy of air power. With so many disadvantages, the B-25 could not fail to be a great success. The US Army Air Corps ordered the new aircraft off the drawing-board and the first production machine flew on 19 August 1940. The initial model (B-25) had constant dihedral wings, but stability problems were solved by making the outboard wing panels

ABOVE: *The B-25 was one of the most popular and versatile twin-engined aircraft of the war. The B-25J shown here had the astonishing armament fit of 18 0.5in Browning machine guns.*

LEFT: *A North American B-25 Mitchell during a raid against a Japanese installation. Note the gull wing, which was developed after stability problems were experienced with the early prototypes by removing the dihedral from the outboard wing sections.*

horizontal, giving the aircraft its characteristic "gull-wing" appearance (B-25A).

The B-25B, which entered service in 1941, had a different defensive armament, including a retractable ventral turret, which proved troublesome and was later deleted. Nevertheless, the B-25B was a very effective aircraft and was supplied to the USAAC and to Allies, including Great Britain and the Free French. It was also one of the first US aircraft to be supplied in significant numbers to the Soviet Union, being ferried by US aircrews to Teheran in Persia, where Soviet crews took over.

RIGHT: *The success of the Tokyo Raid gave its leader, Lt Col James Doolittle, a strong feeling for the B-25 Mitchell. When he was promoted to general he adopted the example shown here as his personal aircraft.*

BELOW: *Doolittle's B-25Bs on the deck of the carrier, USS* Hornet, *en route to the launch position for the Tokyo Raid. Due to their size, the B-25s could not be struck-down in the hangar, while the forward aircraft had a much shorter take-off run than those at the stern.*

LEFT: *Close-up showing the lashings securing one of the B-25s' nosewheels to the flightdeck. Despite the long voyage on the open flight-deck not one aircraft suffered a mechanical malfunction.*

RIGHT: *Japanese naval base in Tokyo Bay seen from one of Doolittle's B-25s. The Japanese defenders were taken by surprise, showing themselves to be less than ready to protect the homeland*

BELOW RIGHT: *Lt Col Doolittle and Admiral Mitscher aboard USS* Hornet *with some of the aircrew who would take part in the raid – not all of these very brave men would survive.*

BELOW: *The pilot hauls one of the first B-25s off the flightdeck of USS* Hornet; *in fact, he is well off the deck as he flies over the bows. All 16 B-25s took off from the deck successfully.*

DOOLITTLE RAID: 18 APRIL 1942.

One of the most imaginative air operations in history was conceived by a US Navy submariner, who had the idea of carrier-borne bombers striking at the Japanese homeland. The idea was approved at the highest level and execution assigned to Lieutenant-Colonel James H. Doolittle, a skilled pilot and noted engineer, who went to the most experienced B-25 unit, 17th Bombardment Group, to ask for volunteers for an unspecified mission. He was overwhelmed with the response and was able to select 24 crews. The aircraft themselves were B-25Bs, but with the ventral turret, Norden bombsights and any superfluous equipment removed and extra fuel tanks added, while brand-new propellers were also installed. Thus equipped, crews and aircraft flew to San Francisco where they embarked aboard the carrier USS *Hornet,* which sailed on 1 April with 16 B-25s lashed to the deck.

It was planned to launch the bombers some 400 miles (645km) from the Japanese coast, but on the morning of 18 April the radar of the carrier Enterprise, which was escorting Hornet, located a Japanese ship forming part of a picket line 700 miles (1,126km) off the Japanese coast. Unable to risk two of the US Navy's precious carriers, Admiral Halsey, in overall command of the operation, ordered the immediate launch (a decision with which Doolittle fully agreed). Hornet steamed at full speed into a 27-knot gale and all B-25s took-off safely, each overloaded aircraft clawing its way into the sky and every pilot making his first carrier take-off.

By then the Japanese had been warned of the bombers' approach and several were intercepted by fighters but all the aircraft managed to bomb their designated targets and to escape westwards towards China. All but one arrived over Japanese-occupied China but the crews were forced to bale out when their aircraft ran out of fuel, while one aircraft landed at Vladivostok, where the crew was promptly interned by their Soviet allies. Eight men were captured by the Japanese, of which four were-tried, convicted and executed for bombing civilians, something the Japanese themselves had been doing in China for a decade.

The actual damage inflicted on the Japanese cities was not great but the raid was a tremendous boost for US morale, while it was the first demonstration to the Japanese that their revered homeland would never be safe from the long reach of the United States. It was a major loss of face for the Imperial Japanese Navy and Army which had so obviously failed to defend the homeland.

NORTH AMERICAN P-51D MUSTANG

SPECIFICATIONS

COUNTRY OF ORIGIN: United States of America.

TYPE: single-seat fighter.

MANUFACTURER: North American Aviation Inc

IN SERVICE: 1941–1945.

WEIGHTS: empty 7,125lb (3,230kg); loaded 11,600lb (5,206kg).

DIMENSIONS: span 37.0ft (11.3m); length 32.2ft (9.8m); height 13.7ft (4.1m).

ENGINE : 1 x Packard V-1650-7 vee-12 liquid-cooled, in-line engine, 1,590hp (licence-built Rolls-Royce Merlin 61-series).

PERFORMANCE: max speed 437mph (703km/h); initial climb 3,475ft/min (1,060m/min); service ceiling 41,900ft (12,770m); combat range 950 miles (1,530km); operational range with drop tanks 1,300 miles (2,100km); absolute range to dry tanks 2,080 miles (3,350km).

WEAPONS: 6 x 0.5in Browning MG53-2 (270 or 400 rounds each); two 1,000lb (4,54kg) bombs on wing racks.

DESIGN HISTORY

In April 1940 British aircraft designers and factories were fully stretched meeting the RAF's requirements, so the British turned to the United States' North American company for help in designing and building a completely new, heavily armed and fast fighter, intended primarily for operations over 20,000ft (6,100m). It took the company just 117 days for the prototype to fly (26 October 1940). The sleek, low-wing monoplane was powered by an Allison V-1710 engine (1,125hp) and armed with four 0.5in Browning machine guns; it was immediately ordered for the RAF as the Mustang I, while the US Army joined in with an order for 500 as the A-36A and 310 as the P-51A.

TOP: *P-51B of 334th Fighter Squadron with Malcolm bubble hood in place of the earlier hinged pattern.*

ABOVE: *P-51D of 8th Air Force's 361st Fighter Group in late 1944, operating out of St Dizier, France.*

RIGHT: *P-51B of 355th Fighter Squadron with two underwing fuel tanks, giving much greater range.*

These early versions were excellent, but were better at low rather than high level and were usually employed as fighter-bombers. The full potential of the design was, however, only realised when it was re-engined with the combat-proven Rolls-Royce Merlin engine (licence-built in the United States by Packard) and entered service with the RAF as the Mustang II and the USAAF as the P-51B. Next came the P-51C/Mustang III with a bulged hood and then the definitive P-51D/Mustang IV with a bubble canopy, cut-down rear fuselage, dorsal fin and six 0.5in machine guns, which re-equipped USAAF Mustang wings in the European theatre in autumn 1944.

ABOVE: *P-51D of 352nd Fighter Squadron of 353rd Fighter Group, 8th Air Force, returns safely to its base at Raydon, England, after a bomber escort operation over mainland Europe.*

RIGHT: *The first North American Mustangs were powered by the Allison V-1710 1,150hp engine, but its power fell off with increased altitude. These aircraft were later designated A-36A (as here) and used in the ground-attack role.*

LONG-RANGE BOMBER ESCORT: 1944–1945.

In north-west Europe the main mission of the USAAF strategic bomber force was to conduct daylight raids against targets in central Europe and the further these raids extended into the Third Reich the greater the number of fighters the *Luftwaffe* was able to use against them. The bombers – B-17 Fortresses and B-24 Liberators – bristled with defensive weapons, and tactics were constantly being refined to maximise their mutual support. But losses were high and the only real solution lay in fighters escorting them all the way "there-and-back" and in being able to engage in combat at any stage. Such cover was gradually extended by P-38s and P-47s, but it was the P-51 which provided the full solution. On 6 March 1944 P-51Cs of the 4th Fighter Group escorted B-17 bombers all the way to Berlin and back, and from then on regularly appeared over the German capital.

The P-51C and the later P-51D could more than hold their own against German propeller-driven aircraft but the new types introduced by the *Luftwaffe* in 1944 provided new challenges. The Messerschmitt 163 was first encountered on 28 July 1944 and this revolutionary rocket-propelled fighter had a considerable speed advantage, even over the P-51D, but was hampered by a very short endurance. At first the Me-163s inflicted some losses on the P-51s but tactics were soon evolved which brought the threat within bearable limits.

From September 1944 onwards, however, yet another new enemy appeared in the shape of the Messerschmitt 262, powered by two turbojets; this was not as fast as the Me 163, but had much greater endurance and was better armed. Even so, the P-51s held their own and regularly shot down Me 262s, the first two being downed on 9 October 1944 and the best day being 24 March 1945 when aircraft of 31st Fighter Group, escorting bombers to Berlin, shot down five Me 262s and one Me 163.

The Mustang was one of the most valuable aircraft on the strength of the USAAF and by VE-Day (8 May 1945) 354th Fighter Group had destroyed 701 enemy aircraft in 17 months of combat, the highest score by any group in the whole USAAF.

ABOVE: *Ship 44-13704 "Ferocious Frankie" carrying two 1,000lb (454kg) under-wing bombs on a ground-attack mission, a secondary task for this superb fighter.*

LEFT: *The North American P-51D Mustang was one of the finest fighters of World War II, its long range making a major difference to the Allied strategic bombing campaign over Germany.*

RIGHT: *Ship 44-13357, named "Tika IV" by its pilot, was an early model P-51D of 374th Fighter Squadron of 361st Fighter Group. Like other early Ds, it later had a dorsal fin added to increase directional stability.*

BATTLE-WINNING WARSHIPS

THE NAVAL TREATIES

An important influence on the size and composition of the major navies in World War II, and on the characteristics of their larger ships, were the naval treaties signed in the inter-war years. The first of these, signed in Washington in 1920, included numerous limits on the size and composition of the world's battle fleets, among which was a 10-year ban on battleship construction. (One Japanese and three US battleships already under construction were allowed to be completed, and, to achieve balance, Britain would be allowed to build two new battleships.) Limits were also agreed on the maximum displacement of certain classes: battleships – 35,000 tons; aircraft carriers – 27,000 tons (but two could be 33,000 tons); and all other ships – 10,000 tons. Limits were also placed on armament calibres: 16in (406mm) for battleships and 8in (203mm) for all others. A second conference was held in London in 1930, where further limits were agreed, but both these agreements were due to end in 1936, so a further conference was convened in London in 1935.

Germany naval power was limited by the Versailles Treaty (1919) which limited the size of the navy to 15,000 men and eight antiquated pre-dreadnoughts, eight light cruisers, 16 destroyers and 16 torpedo boats. Strict limits were also placed on new construction, and no submarines or naval aircraft were permitted. Germany was excluded from the Washington and London naval conferences, but in 1935 came to an agreement with Great Britain under which the *Kriegsmarine* was allowed to operate 35 per cent of the British tonnage in surface warships and 45 per cent (later 100 per cent) in submarines.

These agreements were well-intentioned, but some navies flouted their terms. The agreements collapsed one after another in the mid-1930s and, by the time of the outbreak of war in Europe in 1939, the majority of navies had large-scale building programmes in hand.

THE TRADITIONAL MEASURE OF NAVAL POWER

At the start of World War II the power of the leading navies (ie, those of France, Germany, Great Britain, Italy, Japan, and the United States) was judged by the traditional measure: the size and effectiveness of their battleship and battlecruiser fleets.* There were some engagements between such ships during the early war years, for example, *Bismarck* versus *Hood*, but never a major fleet action on the lines of Jutland in 1916. Instead, the limits of battleship power were shown by the destruction of the US Pacific fleet in port by Japanese carrier-based

aircraft at Pearl Harbor (7 December 1941) and of the British battleship *Prince of Wales* and battlecruiser *Repulse* at sea by Japanese land-based aircraft (10 December 1941). Thereafter, although battleships remained very active throughout the war, their power and influence waned rapidly and by 1944 their main importance lay in the provision of anti-aircraft fire, especially against kamikaze attacks, and shore bombardment.

THE NEW MEASURE OF NAVAL POWER

The new capital ship was the aircraft carrier, although throughout the war only Great Britain, Japan and the United States operated significant air arms; Germany and Italy started work on such ships, but did not complete any. Carrier-borne aircraft quickly demonstrated the capabilities of aircraft carriers, the most telling early example being the British attack on the Italian fleet in Taranto (12 November 1940). However, that action was overshadowed by the attack on Pearl Harbor in which Japanese carrier aircraft dealt a devastating defeat on the United States battle fleet, although, crucially, they were unable to find the American carriers. Those US carriers, which were safely at sea, and their successors, which were built in large numbers, became one of the most important ingredients in defeating the Japanese.

Aircraft carriers were not, in themselves, battle-winners, but it was the carrier that took the aircraft to the place from where they could be launched and recovered. Thus, while the words "Pearl Harbor" conjure up pictures of Japanese aircraft diving and wheeling above the US Pacific Fleet, the could not have got there without the *Shokaku* and the other carriers, lying unseen over the horizon, which had taken them close to their target and which subsequently took them on to further actions elsewhere.

TWO SUBMARINE WARS

Two quite different submarine wars were fought, and in each case one single class predominated throughout the war. In the case of the US Navy this was the Gato/Balao-class, whose boats were responsible for sinking a large number of surface warships in the Pacific war and for the virtually annihilation of the Japanese merchant fleet. In the Atlantic, German U-boats caused great destruction, as they had in World War I, with the attack being led by the Type VII. These boats caused great havoc in the years 1939-1942 and brought the British to the verge of defeat, and then went on to carry out a devastating attack on the United States' East Coast in the first half of 1942.

CRUISERS

The size and armament of cruisers had been limited by the Washington and London treaties to 10,000 tons and 8in (203mm) guns, giving rise to what were known as "Treaty cruisers", such as the US Pensacola-class and the British Kent-class. The Germans, however, were limited by the Versailles Treaty which had ended World War I. This restricted them to a maximum of 10,000 tons and 11in (280mm) guns. However, they built three ships which supposedly just met the treaty limits, but which, as was later discovered, actually exceeded them by a considerable margin. These were known as *panzerschiffe* (armoured ships) in Germany and as "pocket battleships" in Britain and the USA. The first major naval engagement of the war was between one of these ships, *Admiral Graf Spee*, and three British cruisers at the Battle of the River Plate. Once the various treaty limits were abandoned, however, larger cruisers were built, and such ships played an important role on both sides in the Pacific war.

THE DASHING DESTROYERS

Virtually all navies operated destroyers, which performed a multiplicity of duties, ranging from escorting battleships, through anti-submarine escort to independent actions. The majority were well-armed and fast, and, under the right commander, had an air of "dash" about them. As was shown by the British Onslow-class at the Battle of the Barents Sea (31 December 1942) and the United States' Fletcher-class at the Battle of Savo Island (13 November 1942), they could take part in actions with much larger ships and not only survive but also play a major part in the resulting success.

THE LONGEST BATTLE

Battleships, aircraft carriers and cruisers were large, visually impressive and had an aura of power, while destroyers made up for their smaller size by their dash and aggression. But there were even smaller and humbler ships which also played vital roles and won their own battles, most particularly in the anti-submarine war. These small warships were classified variously as destroyer-escorts, sloops, frigates or corvettes, and they patrolled day after day from September 1939 to May 1945, attempting to defend the convoys so vital to Britain's survival. Smallest of these were the British corvettes, which were little more than armed whaling ships, with light armament and poor sensors. Yet without them and their courageous crews – largely reservists – the Battle of the Atlantic could well have been lost in the first three years of the war.

AMPHIBIOUS WARFARE SHIPS

The great amphibious landings, such as those in Sicily, Normandy and the Pacific islands are remembered, quite properly, for the actual landings, the battles on the beaches and the subsequent breakouts. But, without the unglamorous amphibious warfare vessels such as the Tank Landing Craft, the Allied armies and all their equipment would never have reached those beaches in the first place.

"HUMAN TORPEDOES"

One of the most outstanding contributions to the war at sea came from the Italian Navy, whose frogmen, one-man motorboats and two-man torpedoes did damage out of all proportion to their numbers.

---

*The distinction originated in the early 1900s when a battleship had maximum firepower and protection, but compromised on speed, while a battlecruiser had maximum firepower and speed, but compromised on protection. Some battlecruisers continued to serve in World War II (for example, the British *Hood*, German *Scharnhorst*) but the distinction became largely academic with the advent of the fast battleship (for example, German *Bismarck*, United States' *Iowa*) which had heavy firepower, good protection and high speed.

BISMARCK

SPECIFICATIONS

COUNTRY OF ORIGIN: Germany.

TYPE: battleship.

COMMISSIONED: 24 August 1940.

DISPLACEMENT: standard 41,700 tons; full load 50,900 tons.

DIMENSIONS: length 823.5ft (251m); beam 118.1ft (36m); draught 33.5ft (10.2m).

PROPULSION: Blohm + Voss geared steam-turbines, 12 Wagner boilers; 138,000shp; 3 shafts; speed 29kt.

ARMOUR: belt 12.6in-8.7in (320-220mm); decks 2in + 3.2-4.7in (50mm + 8–120mm); turrets 14.1-7.0in (360–180mm).

WEAPONS: 8 x 15in (380mm) (4 x 2); 12 x 5.9in (150mm) (6 x 2); 16 x 4.1in (105mm) (8 x 2) AA; 16 x 37mm (8 x 2) AA; 12 x 20mm AA.

AIRCRAFT: 6 x Arado Ar-234 catapult-launched floatplanes.

COMPLEMENT: 2,092.

DESIGN HISTORY

*B*ismarck and *Tirpitz* were the only true battleships to be completed during the Nazi regime, design work starting on the ships in 1932 and on the new 15in (380mm) guns in 1934, following which *Bismarck* was officially ordered in 1935 and *Tirpitz* in 1936. There were many good points about these very impressive-looking ships. They had a very powerful primary armament of eight 15in (380mm) guns in four twin turrets, with a first-class surface fire-control system, a key element of which was the very accurate optical rangefinders, although the system was also helped by having one of the early radars, fitted in early 1941. The air defence weapons and fire-control systems were also good.

On the other hand, the German Navy, unlike the victors in World War I, had no opportunity during the 1920s and early 1930s to experiment and carry out tests on their old battleships, so they persisted with the system of protection which had served them well at the Battle of Jutland. Thus, by the standards of the late 1930s, the design of the protection system for *Bismarck* was very conservative, being generally similar to that of the Baden-class battleships of 1916,

BELOW: Fresh from its builder's yard, battleship Bismarck *sails serenely in the Baltic in late 1940. It is an impressive sight, its well-balanced shape and massive gun turrets presenting an indelible image of naval power. Used properly it could have presented the British with an intractable problem, but it made just one operational voyage.*

albeit with a slight reduction in the thickness of the side belt and a corresponding increase in the horizontal protection; the belt was also fabricated from the latest nickel-chrome steel.

However, the range at which engagements had taken place had increased very considerably since 1918 so that, while these German battleships were very well protected against comparatively short-range direct shellfire, they were more vulnerable to long-range plunging shells. Also, the main armoured

deck was low down in the hull, resulting in many important compartments higher up being protected by only a thin shield of armour plate. They also had very broad beams, which gave plenty of room for underwater protection and made them steady gun platforms, but which, allied to a low freeboard, made them relatively poor sea boats.

Despite this, *Bismarck* and *Tirpitz* were very strongly built and well sub-divided, and experience was to show that both of them were exceptionally

LEFT: A very impressive sight: battleship Bismarck *at maximum speed of 29 knots in the Baltic on 27 February 1941. The ship was intended to serve as a commerce raider, making regular forays deep into the Atlantic sea-lanes, sinking as many warships and merchantmen as possible, disrupting British convoy schedules and forcing the British Royal Navy to overextend itself.*

ABOVE: Bismarck *as it appeared in May 1941, except that the camouflage lines and bow/ stern wave (intended to disguise its length) were painted out with normal grey; the swastika was retained.*

BELOW: Bismarck *fires a broadside during the night action against the British battlecruiser* Hood, *as seen from the accompanying German*

cruiser, Prinz Eugen. Hood *blew up and sank during the action, with the loss of 95 officers and 1,323 men, just three crewmen being rescued.*

RIGHT: *British battleship* Rodney *shells* Bismarck, *which is burning on the horizon, seeking revenge for the loss of battlecruiser* Hood *in the Denmark Strait, which had been a serious blow to British naval pride.*

BATTLE OF DENMARK STRAIT: 24 MAY 1941

*B*ismarck was commissioned on 24 August 1940, but her commanding officer (Captain Lindemann) took a full eight months to complete the working-up period in the safe waters of the Baltic. Thus, it was not until 18 May 1941 that *Bismarck* sailed from Gotenhafen (formerly Gdynia) on its first (and as it would prove, its only) operational voyage, accompanied by the heavy cruiser *Prinz Eugen* (Captain Brinkmann). The two ships formed a squadron commanded by Admiral Lütjens, flying his flag aboard *Bismarck*. As they passed through the Belts on 20 May they were spotted by the Swedish cruiser, *Gotland*, but they reached the Korsfjord, near Bergen, Norway, at 0900 on 21 May without further incident; they immediately refuelled and sailed for the Atlantic that evening.

The British knew *Bismarck* had completed its working-up period and had expected it to appear in the Atlantic before this, so *Gotland*'s sighting report, which reached London via the British naval attaché in Stockholm, did not come as a surprise. Reconnaissance aircraft quickly found the two ships in the Korsfjord and the Royal Navy's Battlecruiser Squadron, consisting of HMS *Hood*, a 20-years old battlecruiser and the pride of the Royal Navy, HMS *Prince of Wales*, a brand-new battleship, and five destroyers, sailed from Scapa Flow on 21 May, as a precautionary measure.

On 22 May another British reconnaissance aircraft confirmed that the fjord was empty, so, assuming that the German ships were heading for the Altantic, Britain's Home Fleet sailed from Scapa Flow. This force, together with the reinforcements which joined at sea, consisted of one battleship, one battlecruiser, one aircraft carrier, seven cruisers and five destroyers. In addition, two heavy cruisers (HMS Norfolk and Suffolk) patrolled the Denmark Strait, (the narrow gap between Iceland and Greenland), while three light cruisers and five trawlers covered the Iceland-Faroes Gap.

On 23 May *Bismarck* and *Prinz Eugen* were sighted passing through the Denmark Strait, first by *Norfolk* at 1922, followed by *Suffolk* an hour later. The two cruisers started to shadow the Germans as they headed for the open waters of the Atlantic. Aboard *Bismarck* Lütjens knew that they had been found, and was initially surprised by the tenacity of the British cruisers, but he quickly realised that they must be equipped with radar. Despite this, Lütjens maintained his course and at 0320 *Bismarck*'s lookouts spotted the *Hood* and *Prince of Wales* approaching at a range of about 26,000yd (23,800m).

Both sides opened fire at almost the same time, but the superb German optical instruments enabled them to establish the range first, so that the opening salvo against *Hood* was close and the second straddled the British ship. By now the four ships were some 20,000yd (18,300m) apart and *Bismarck*'s third salvo again straddled *Hood*. But this time there was an astonishing development as the startled onlookers saw a flash of flame rise from the British battlecruiser, accompanied by a rumbling noise, following which the ship simply disappeared; 95 officers and 1,323 men were lost in the explosion and just three were rescued. The two German ships now concentrated on the *Prince of Wales* and hits were quickly scored, forcing the British ship, which was suffering from a number of mechanical problems, to turn sharply and break off the action.

All this had been achieved without a single casualty on either of the German ships. *Prinz Eugen* escaped unscathed, but not *Bismarck*, which had been hit twice, one round passing clean through the ship, leaving an exit hole more than 3ft (1m) in diameter, while the other exploded inside the ship causing considerable damage and starting a fuel oil leak. As a result, *Bismarck* had a 9 degree list to port and maximum speed was restricted to 28 knots, so Lütjens decided to release *Prinz Eugen* to carry on with its anti-commerce mission, while he took his flagship to German-occupied St Nazaire in France for repairs.

Lütjens calculated that he would reach the French port on 28 May, but the British brought up reinforcements and hunted down the ship that had demolished the beloved *Hood*. Harassed by shadowing cruisers and destroyers, and attacked by Swordfish aircraft, *Bismarck* was finally destroyed by battleships, sinking on 27 May with the loss of 2,106 men.

In the Battle of Denmark Strait, *Bismarck* showed two of the great strengths of German battleship design: heavy firepower coordinated by an excellent fire control system. These enabled it to take advantage of one of the known weaknesses of British battlecruiser design – inadequate protection, especially against long-range, plunging fire – although quite what caused the *Hood* to blow-up so suddenly and so catastrophically is now impossible to establish. Nevertheless, at the end of this very brief encounter *Bismarck* and *Prinz Eugen* had won a remarkable victory. *Hood*, the most glamorous ship in the Royal Navy, which for 20 years had been the epitome of naval power, had been sunk, and *Prince of Wales*, the newest battleship in the British fleet, was forced to leave the scene.

SCHARNHORST, GNEISENAU

DESIGN HISTORY

These two ships almost invariably served in company and are therefore described together. The German Navy's first major warship programme following World War I was for five Deutschland-class *panzerschiffe* (= armoured ships), the design concept being that they would outgun any ship that could catch them and outrun any ship with a heavier armament. The appearance in the mid-1930s of fast battleships, such as the French Dunquerque-class, rendered this concept obsolete and the programme was terminated with the third ship, and a larger, faster and more powerful design was prepared.

The main armament of this new design was intended to be three triple 15in (380mm) guns, but as these were not ready it was decided to take the four triple 11in (208mm) turrets already built for the cancelled fourth and fifth Deutschland-class and to build two more, enabling the new ships to have three triple 11in (208mm) each. It was planned to replace these with 15in (380mm) turrets in due course, but this never happened.

Diesels, as used in the Deutschland-class, could not provide the power required, so a novel design of lightweight, high-pressure, superheated steam propulsion was installed instead. This was rushed into service without proper development, and

proved to be complicated and fault-prone, while the use of turbines rather than diesels meant a substantial reduction in range.

These two ships certainly looked impressive, but their major weakness was the main armament, since any enemy battleship, even an old one, could deliver far heavier shells over a much greater range than the 11in (208mm) guns. As a result, both *Scharnhorst* and *Gneisenau* always declined an engagement with a British battleship, and were effectively confined to the raiding role.

RIGHT: *Scharnhorst's sister ship,* Gneisenau, *photographed near a Norwegian port in late 1940. The battlecruisers acted as a team in commerce raids.*

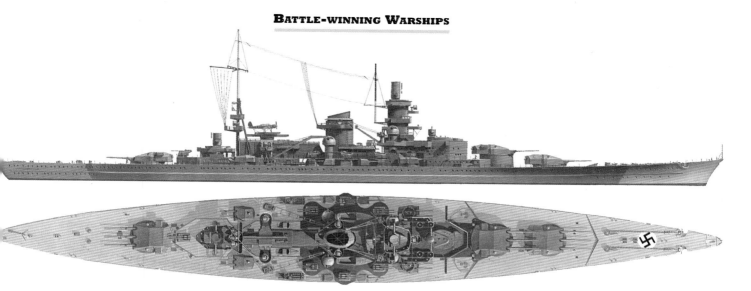

THE "CHANNEL DASH": 10 FEBRUARY 1942.

*S*charnhorst and *Gneisenau* sortied into the North Atlantic in November 1939 and in April 1940 they took part in the invasion of Norway. In a brief action with the British battlecruiser *Renown*, *Gneisenau* sustained three 15in (380mm) hits. In June they encountered the British carrier *Glorious* which they sank, together with its two accompanying destroyers. In January 1941 both ships carried out a 60-day raid in the Atlantic, during the course of which they sank 22 ships (115,000grt), subsequently entering Brest, where they were heavily bombed, *Scharnhorst* receiving five hits. It was eventually decided that they should return to Germany, accompanied by the heavy cruiser, *Prinz Eugen*, which had entered the port after its foray with Bismarck (see separate entry).

The original plan was for these three ships to return to Germany northabout around the British Isles, but Hitler insisted on the more daring plan of proceeding straight up the Channel. Named Operation Cerberus, the naval force comprised *Scharnhorst*, *Gneisenau*, and *Prinz Eugen* escorted by six destroyers, which were later joined by 14 torpedo boats and three flotillas of MTBs; air support was provided by Luftflotte 3.

The main element sailed from Brest in the late evening of 10 February 1942 and even though the British suspected that the Germans would try a Channel transit they were very slow to react. The German ships were off Le Touquet before being spotted and the first real reaction was from coastal guns at Ramsgate. This was followed by attacks by MTBs from Dover and Ramsgate, Swordfish from Manston and then by destroyers from Harwich, but all proved ineffective. The only setback came off the Dutch coast, when *Scharnhorst* hit two mines and *Gneisenau* one, but both reached their destination ports without difficulty.

Operation Cerberus was a major tactical success, causing deep embarrassment to the British, but in the longer term it proved to be a strategic defeat since *Gneisenau* and *Prinz Eugen* never again played a significant role in the war, although *Scharnhorst* was eventually deployed to Norway, where it was sunk in the Battle of the North Cape in December 1943. The key to the success of Cerberus was the speed of the ships, their ability to absorb the mine damage and the unusually good coordination between the German naval and air forces.

LEFT: Gneisenau *leads* Scharnhorst *out of a Norwegian fjord. They caused the British great problems until they were trapped in Brest.*

BELOW: *A torpedo boat leads* Scharnhorst, Gneisenau *and* Prinz Eugen *in the "Channel Dash", a German success which severely embarrassed the British.*

TOP: Scharnhorst, *December 1943. Because the intended 15in (380mm) guns were not ready it was armed with nine 11in (280mm) guns, the weapons of a heavy cruiser.*

S-BOOT – S38 IMPROVED CLASS

DESIGN HISTORY

These highly effective craft were known to the Allies as "E-boats", but to the Germans they were *Schnellboote* (*S-boote* = fast boats). Prototypes were built by various yards in the 1920s, from which the Lürssen design was selected and it then remained in production for some 15 years, incorporating some minor improvements in the process. Main armament in all groups were two 21in (533mm) torpedo tubes, initially mounted on the open foredeck, but from the S26 group onwards the foredeck level was raised to enclose the tubes. Two reloads were carried by all groups. All *S-boote* carried guns, originally a single 20mm cannon, mounted amidships, later increased

to two single 20mm or one twin 20mm; a 40mm gun was added later.

The first six boats were powered by three petrol

SPECIFICATIONS

COUNTRY OF ORIGIN: Germany.
TYPE: motor torpedo boat.
COMMISSIONED: 1943–1945.
DISPLACEMENT: 100 tons standard; 117 tons deep load.
DIMENSIONS: length 114.6ft (34.9m); beam 16.8ft (5.1m); draught 5.0ft (1.5m).
PROPULSION: three shafts; three Daimler-Benz diesels; 7,5000bhp; speed 42kt.
WEAPONS: 1 x 20mm, 1 x 40mm cannon; 2 x 21in (533m) torpedo tubes, plus 2 reloads.
COMPLEMENT: 21.

ABOVE: *Two of the S-38 group, seen here in 1945, showing the* panzerkalotte (= *armoured bridge) which was fitted to S-67 and later boats to provide protection for the bridge crew.*

RIGHT: *These formidable MTBs were known as* Schnellboote (S-boote [= fast boats]) *to the Germans and as "E-boats" by the Allies.*

RIGHT: *S-4, one of the second batch, built in 1932. These had a low foredeck and flush deck, with the torpedo tubes in an open mount (compare with the raised forecastle and enclosed tubes in the artwork below). Note also the pre-Hitler naval ensign.*

BATTLE OF SLAPTON SANDS: 4/5 APRIL 1944.

In mid-1942 the *Kriegsmarine* decided to exploit the vulnerability of the British Western Channel and from then on maintained at least one *S-boote* flotilla in Cherbourg, France, tasked with conducting offensive operations against Allied coastal convoy routes. These flotillas conducted regular forays across the Channel, inflicting losses, disrupting the convoy schedules and forcing the British to deploy resources to deal with this small but aggravating threat.

Prior to the D-day landings, Allied forces conducted a series of amphibious exercises, starting in early March 1944. Exercise Tiger, held in April, involved an amphibious force spending one night at sea in Lyme Bay, on the southern coast of England, to simulate the cross-Channel voyage before landing its troops on Slapton Sands. This involved convoys of LSts (Landing Ships Tank), their slow speed making them particularly vulnerable to enemy action.

Convoy T4 comprised eight LSTs carrying US Engineer Corps troops, escorted (in theory) by an elderly destroyer, HMS *Scimitar*, and a modern but slow (maximum speed 16kt) corvette, HMS *Azalea*, neither of which had any previous experience against *S-boote*. In the early hours of 4 April, however, *Scimitar* was forced to return to Plymouth following a collision, where the dockyard refused to allow it to sail.

Due to a series of misunderstandings, however, *Scimitar's*

non-appearance was not reported until 1900 and it was not until 0200 on 5 April that another destroyer was ordered to join the convoy. Meanwhile, the eight LSTs of convoy T4 were proceeding in line ahead at a speed of 3.5kt, their sole escort, *Azalea*, a mile ahead, a position more suitable for its customary ASW role than for protection against *S-boote*.

Nine *S-boote* of 5th and 9th Flotillas sailed from Cherbourg at 2000 on 4 April and passed through various British patrol lines without being detected, their first contact being with a destroyer, HMS *Onslow*, which the Germans attacked just after midnight. It escaped without damage.

In Lyme Bay the S-boote found the tail-end of convoy T4, their first target being LST507 which was hit at 0203, burst into flames and then sank, followed by LST531, which blew apart in a massive explosion. There was then a general melee, with LSTs blundering around and with numerous cases of "blue-on-blue" firing in the darkness. The S-boote scored one more hit, on LST296, (which lost its stern but did not sink), but their score might have been greater had they realised earlier that their targets were shallow draught vessels and re-set the depth controls on their torpedoes accordingly. As it was, their attack had a devastating effect (two LSTs sunk, one damaged, 749 killed) and in the longer term almost caused the D-day landings to be postponed.

engines, but such inflammable fuel was unsuitable for the boats' role and diesels were installed from the seventh boat onwards. All hulls were of round bilge design, the only substantial change being a prominent knuckle, introduced in the eighth and subsequent boats. This round bilge was

both seaworthy and generated little wake, making them hard to locate at night.

A total of 249 *S-boote* were built for the *Kriegsmarine*, of which 157 were either sunk in action or scuttled at the war's end, leaving 92 to be surrendered to the Allies in 1945.

LEFT: *S-80 series boat. Weapons carried include two torpedo tubes (in the forecastle), depth-charge rails aft, one 40mm gun aft and one 20mm cannon in the bows. Note the unarmoured bridge (compare with photographs).*

U-BOAT TYPE VIIC

DESIGN HISTORY

The Type VII U-boat was one of those weapons systems which possess not one outstanding attribute and yet prove to be an excellent compromise. Thus, its shortcomings included too few weapons, insufficient range, low underwater speed and an acutely uncomfortable life for the number of men required to man all its systems. However, it proved relatively easy to manufacture, could be produced in large numbers, and in the right hands it proved to be a deadly efficient killing machine. There were a number of versions of the Type VII but by far the most numerous was the Type VIIC, of which 593 were commissioned, plus a further 70 of an improved version, the Type VIIC/42.

ABOVE: *U-744 comes alongside at the end of a mission. The Type VIIC bore the brunt of the U-boat war in the Atlantic and remained in production to the very end.*

BELOW: *Three Type VIICs (with one Type IX on left) lie at Wilhelmshaven after the surrender in 1945. Type VIIC losses were heavy and these men were lucky to survive.*

SPECIFICATIONS

COUNTRY OF ORIGIN: Germany.
TYPE: attack submarine.
COMMISSIONED: 1940–1945.
DISPLACEMENT: surfaced 761tons; submerged 865 tons.
DIMENSIONS: length (67.1m); beam (6.2m); draught (4.8m).
PROPULSION: two shafts; two diesels, 1,400hp; two electric motors, 375hp; speed 17.0kt (surfaced), 7.6kt (submerged).
DIVING DEPTH: operational 330ft (100m); crush 660ft (200m).
WEAPONS: original – one 88mm, one 20mm; later – one 37mm, one twin 20mm; torpedo tubes: bow – four 533mm; stern – one 533mm; torpedoes carried – 14; mines: 26 x TMA or 39 x TMB (in lieu of torpedoes).
COMPLEMENT: 44.

BATTLE OF THE ATLANTIC: 1939–1945

U-402, a Type VIIC, and its only commanding officer, Siegfried von Forstner, were typical of the U-boat arm and its commanders. Commissioned on 21 May 1941, *U-402* left Bremen on its first operational voyage on 26 October and after joining three successive "wolf packs" it reached Saint Nazaire, France, on 9 December 1941. Its second patrol (11 January–11 February 1942) took it south to the Azores where Forstner damaged a troopship, but the third patrol (26 March–20 May 1942) found *U-402* off the east coast of the United States, serving as part of Operation Drumbeat. During this operation, on 13 April it sank its first victim, *Empire Progress*, followed quickly by the Russian ship, *Ashkabad*, and the third, USS *Cythera*, a former yacht pressed into service as an anti-submarine vessel. *Cythera* blew up, killing 69 people and leaving two survivors who were rescued by von Forstner to become the first US Navy prisoners-of-war in World War II.

The fourth patrol (16 June – 5 August) again took *U-402* to the United States' east coast, but after being damaged by a Coast Guard aircraft (14 July) it was forced to return home. The fifth patrol (4 October–20 November) was far more productive, four ships being sunk on 3 November, but the sixth patrol (14 January – 23 February 1943) was even better, netting six victims, the last of them being sunk by the U-boat's last torpedo. Von Forstner carried on shadowing the convoy and was found by US forces who subjected him to seven separate attacks, but, despite damage, *U-402* survived and on his return to France von Forstner was awarded the Knight's Cross. *U-402* was at sea again on 21 April and sank two ships on the night of 11 May, before returning to La Pallice on 26 May.

After a false start, *U-402* sailed on its eighth patrol on 4 September, but, after various adventures, it was sighted on the surface on 13 October by an Avenger from USS *Card* (CVE-11). Von Forstner decided to fight it out on the surface using his AA guns. When a Wildcat appeared, however, von Forstner had no option but to dive, but as he did so the Avenger rushed in and dropped a homing torpedo. *U-402* was hit and sank with all hands.

Von Forstner's score (15 ships, 71,036grt) was not the greatest, but it was because captains like him kept on going to sea that the U-boat campaign continued for so long and the Germans came so close to winning the Battle of the Atlantic. There were other classes of U-boat, but the Type VIIC was by far the most widely used and scored the victories of 1940-41.

BELOW: *Loading a 21in (533mm) torpedo. The Type VIIC had 5 tubes (4 bow, 1 stern) and carried 14 torpedoes, of which 5 were in the tubes and 9 were reloads.*

RIGHT: *The radio antenna stretching to the bow was the U-boats' weakness. Transmissions were monitored by the Allies to locate the boats and to decrypt the text.*

SILURO A LENTA CORSA (SLC)

DESIGN HISTORY

The *Siluro a lenta corsa* (SLC = slow-running torpedo) which was always known to its crews as "*Maiale*" (= pig) from its poor handling qualities, was based on a standard 21in (533mm) torpedo and powered by a 1.6hp electric motor, which gave a maximum speed (with passengers) of 4.5kt over a distance of 4nm (7.4km) although at a lower speed of 2.3kt the range was increased to 15nm (28km).

The SLC had a crew of two, who wore protective rubber suits and were equipped with self-contained underwater breathing apparatus (SCUBA) with a 6-hour oxygen supply. They sat astride the torpedo, their feet in stirrups, the officer/pilot in front behind

BELOW: *Italian submarine Sciré (Commander Prince Borghese) carried three SLCs to Alexandria, where they carried out a very daring and successful attack on the British Fleet.*

BOTTOM: *An SLC was a standard 21in (533mm) torpedo with a crew of two: an officer/pilot who controlled it and a petty officer who assisted the pilot and maintained the machine.*

SPECIFICATIONS

COUNTRY OF ORIGIN: Italy.
TYPE: two-man torpedo.
COMMISSIONED: 1939–1941.
DIMENSIONS: length 22.0ft (6.7m); diameter 21in (533mm).
PROPULSION: one shaft; one electric motor; 1.6hp; speed 4.5kt.
OPERATING depth: 100ft (30m) approx.
WEAPONS: one high explosive warhead 550lb (250kg).
COMPLEMENT: two.

a chest-high, curved metal screen, below which was a control panel with a depth-gauge, level-gauge, compass, and motor controls. Direction and attitude were controlled by a joy-stick, while levers either opened valves to take the craft down or admitted air to bring it to the surface. The petty-officer sat aft, his tasks including maintenance, cutting holes in anti-torpedo nets, and helping place the warhead. This was detachable and contained 550lb (250kg) of high explosive, being detonated by a clockwork-operated fuze with a time delay of up to 5 hours. SLCs were normally carried to the area of their intended operation in containers mounted on the upper deck of a submarine.

ALEXANDRIA, EGYPT: 19 DECEMBER 1941.

The most daring and effective attack carried out by Italian special forces was against the British Mediterranean Fleet in its main base at Alexandria, Egypt. Three SLCs were carried by the submarine *Sciré* (Commander Prince Borghese) to the vicinity of Alexandria harbour entrance, where they were successfully launched. The three SLCs were commanded by Lieutenant (Navy) de la Penne, Captain (Naval Engineer) Marceglia and Captain (Naval Artillery) Martelotta, respectively, each accompanied by a petty officer diver.

Having successfully entered the harbour, the three SLCs headed for their targets. Marceglia was responsible for the fleet flagship, HMS *Queen Elizabeth*, a recently modernized battleship armed with eight 15in (381mm) guns. Marceglia placed the warhead successfully, set the fuze and then, together with his crewman, made his way ashore, where they were captured three days later.

De la Penne's target was HMS *Valiant*, sister-ship to the *Queen Elizabeth*, and he suffered several mishaps. First, his breathing apparatus failed, which forced him to the surface inside the harbour. Then, having repaired that, the propeller was fouled and immobilised just short of the target, which meant that the torpedo had to be manhandled the final few yards along the bottom. Having set the fuze the two men surfaced alongside *Valiant*, were captured, and taken aboard the British battleship where they resisted interrogation and were then imprisoned deep in *Valiant's* hull, where, despite knowing that they were very close to the charges, they remained silent until the explosion occurred at 0620. Martelotta also placed his charge under his correct target, the laden tanker, *Sagona* (7,554 tons). He and his crewman then escaped ashore, where they were eventually captured.

All three warheads were correctly placed and the charges detonated correctly, causing an immense amount of damage. *Queen Elizabeth* had serious damage to machinery and its double bottom stoved in over an area of 5,400 sq ft (502 sq m)

the resultant flooding causing it to settle on the bottom. It was patched up and despatched to the USA for repairs which were completed in June 1943. *Valiant* had a 1,800 sq ft (167 sq m) hole blown in its bottom and considerable internal damage and was out of action until June 1942. *Sagona* was seriously damaged but, as an unexpected bonus to the Italians, the destroyer *Jervis*, which was moored alongside, was also damaged.

In this operation, two battleships were put completely out-of-action for six months and 18 months, respectively, and serious damage was inflicted on a tanker and a destroyer. This completely reversed the balance of naval power in the Mediterranean and was a success that an admiral commanding a fleet at sea would have been proud to achieve, but in this case it was inflicted by six men – three junior officers and three petty officers – and three "human torpedoes".

ABOVE: *The 2-man crew – officer forward, petty officer aft – carry out a surface run aboard their SLC; for submerged work they wore "frogman suits" and breathing apparatus. At maximum speed of 4.5 knots range was 4nm (7.4km), but at a lower speed range could be extended to 15nm (28km).*

LEFT: *The first SLC "mother-ship", Gondar, showing the SLC containers. Gondar undertook the first operation against Alexandria in September 1940, which was aborted when it was learnt that there were no targets.*

I-58

SPECIFICATIONS

COUNTRY OF ORIGIN: Japan.
TYPE: kaiten-carrying submarine.
LAUNCHED: 1944.
DISPLACEMENT: surfaced 2,607 tons; submerged 3,688 tons.
DIMENSIONS: length 356.5ft (108.7m); beam 30.5ft (9.3m); draught 17.0ft (5.2m).
PROPULSION: two shafts; two diesels, 4,700hp; two electric motors, 1,200hp; speed surfaced 18.0kt, submerged 6.5kt.
MAXIMUM operating depth: 330ft (100m).
WEAPONS: 1 x 5.5in (140mm); 2 x 25mm (1 x 2); 6 x 21in (533mm) torpedo tubes; 19 torpedoes.
KAITEN: four.
COMPLEMENT: 94.

DESIGN HISTORY

Some of the submarines operated by the Imperial Japanese Navy during World War II were by far the largest in any contemporary navy. The B3 class, for example, to which I-58 belonged, were 357ft (109m) long and displaced 3,688 tons, compared with 220ft (67m) and 851 tons for the German Type

BELOW: Japanese Navy submarine I-58 had a surface range of 21,000nm at 16kt. Its most momentous success was the sinking of the cruiser, USS Indianapolis (CA-35) on 29 July 1945.

RIGHT: A major prize for the Imperial Japanese Navy late in the war was the USS Indianapolis, *which apparently failed to take evasive action against enemy submarines.*

VIIC, and 312ft (95m) and 1,525 tons for the US Gato-class.

The three-strong B3 class, launched in 1943-44 was optimised for surface range, which was 21,000nm at 16kt, with an endurance of 90 days. As built, these submarines had an aircraft hangar and catapult, while main armament was a single 5.5in (140mm) gun, but these were removed in early 1945 to create the deck space required for four kaiten (suicide torpedoes).

SINKING THE INDIANAPOLIS: 27 JULY 1945

The Japanese submarine fleet was far less successful in World War II than had been expected and failed to justify the high hopes the navy had of it and the resources poured into it. It was, therefore, ironic that one of the submarine service's most spectacular sinkings should have taken place in the very last weeks of the war, at a time when it was all irrelevant, and which initiated a series of controversies which reverberate to this day.

I-58 (Lieutenant-Commander Hashimoto) sailed from Japan on 18 July 1945, its mission being to patrol the Philippine Sea, seeking targets for its kaiten. Just before midnight on 29 July the boat was proceeding submerged with Hashimoto observing through his periscope when, to his astonishment, the bright moonlight revealed a large and unescorted enemy warship coming towards him, at speed and on a steady course. There was no need to deploy the kaiten and Hashimoto launched a spread of six Long Lance torpedoes, three of which hit the target, which was thought to be a battleship.

In fact, the victim was USS *Indianapolis* (Captain McVay), a heavy cruiser, which had just delivered the detonator for the first atomic bomb used against Hiroshima to the island of Tinian. Having delivered it safely Indianapolis set out for Leyte to rejoin the Pacific Fleet and because the air, surface and submarine threat was considered minimal McVay was instructed to travel at speed, zigzagging only if necessary. Although US naval intelligence staffs knew, from decrypting enemy radio messages, that enemy submarines were operating in the Philippine Sea, this was not passed on to McVay, and since his ship was not fitted with sonar and he had no ASW escorts, he was totally unaware of *I-58's* presence .

The first the Americans knew was when their ship was hit by three Long Lance torpedoes. *Indianapolis* sank in three minutes, her propellers still turning to drive it down. It is estimated that some 800 of the 1,119-man crew survived the sinking, but Indianapolis had been unable to send a radio message that it was sinking and, astonishingly, the US authorities failed to realise that the ship was overdue. As a result the men spent three days in the water and only 316 were alive when rescuers finally reached them.

Captain McVay was court-martialled, charged with having failed to zig-zag, and in an unparalleled action Hashimoto was taken to the United States from Japan to give evidence against him. McVay was found guilty but was given the comparatively light sentence of a loss in seniority on the captains' roster. The tragedy lived with him, however, and he felt his responsibilities deeply. In 1960 he donned full naval uniform and shot himself with his service pistol — he died instantly, *I-58's* last victim. The rights and wrongs of the whole episode remain a contentious issue in the United States to this day, but, while *I-58* may have been the victor in this one-on-one engagement, in the final analysis both sides were losers.

SHOKAKU

SPECIFICATIONS

COUNTRY OF ORIGIN: Japan.
TYPE: aircraft carrier.
LAUNCHED: 1 June 1939.
COMMISSIONED: 8 August 1941.
DISPLACEMENT: 25,675 tons standard; 32,105 tons full load.
DIMENSIONS: length 844.8ft (257.5m); beam 85.3ft (26,0m); draught 29.0ft (8.9m); flightdeck 794 x 95ft (242 x 29m).
PROPULSION: four shafts; four sets geared turbines; eight **KAMPON** boilers; 160,000shp; speed 34kt.
ARMOUR: machinery 1.2in (30mm); magazines 6.5in (165mm); deck 3.9in (100mm).
WEAPONS: 16 x 5in (127mm) (8 x 2); 42 x 25mm AA.
AIRCRAFT: operational maximum 72.
COMPLEMENT: 1,660.

DESIGN HISTORY

The first Japanese "flat-top" was *Hosho*, completed in 1922. By the time of the Japanese attack on Pearl Harbor eight had been produced, no more than two to the same design. The most recently completed were *Shokaku* and *Zuikaku*, both of which were completed in 1941 and which were, in essence, enlarged and greatly improved versions of the previous Hiryu-class. Preceding Japanese carriers had a variety of bridge and funnel arrangements, the earliest with no island at all, and the most recent with a port-side island and starboard funnels, which created dangerous cross-deck air currents.

The Shokaku-class was the first to have a starboard-side island with the horizontally discharging funnels on the same side, although the

LEFT: *The scene aboard a Japanese carrier at about 0615 hours Sunday 7 December 1941 as the crew wave farewell to the departing bombers starting their 275 mile flight to attack the US fleet in Pearl Harbor. Never had massed seaborne airpower been used to such effect and it was the carriers that made it possible.*

RIGHT: Shokaku *survived two bombs at the Battle of the Coral Sea (seen here) and another six bombs at the Battle of Santa Cruz, but was finally sunk by torpedoes from the Gato-class submarine USS* Cavalla *in June 1944.*

BELOW: *The two Shokaku-class aircraft carriers were the most up-to-date carriers in the fleet which attacked Pearl Harbor. They were the first Japanese carriers to have a starboard island, which had been a feature of Western carriers for many years.*

funnels were still not integrated into the island, as was normal in other navies. The Shokaku-class was designed to carry a mixed air wing of 84 aircraft, although experience showed that 72 was the practical maximum for operations. The flightdeck was unarmoured and was fed by three elevators from the double hangars.

PEARL HARBOR: 7 DECEMBER 1941.

In December 1941 the striking element of the Imperial Japanese Navy was the First Naval Air Fleet, commanded by Vice-Admiral Nagumo Chuichi, which comprised six carriers in three divisions: *Akagi* (flagship); *Hiryu*, *Kaga*, *Shokaku*, *Soryu*, and *Zuikaku*. For the Pearl Harbor operation these had a screen of nine destroyers led by the light cruiser, *Abukuma*, and a support force of two battleships and two heavy cruisers. Three submarines also provided long-range reconnaissance, and two further destroyers were responsible for screening-off the US-held island of Midway. In addition, the First Naval Air Fleet was accompanied by a fleet train of eight tankers and supply ships. The six carriers had 423 aircraft embarked.

The carrier force and the train completed its assembly in Hittokappu Bay in the Kurile islands (then Japanese) on 22 November 1941 and sailed on 26 November, proceeding slowly eastwards through bad weather and under complete radio silence, its progress being coordinated with the diplomatic negotiations in Washington and Tokyo. By 3 December the force was some 900nm north of Midway island and it altered course to the south-east. Later, the operational ships parted from the train and proceeded due south until they reached a point some 275nm north of Pearl Harbor where at 0600 on Sunday 7 December the flagship hoisted the flag "Z" as the signal for the aircraft launch to commence. The actual flag used was the one with which Admiral Togo had signalled the attack on the Russians at Tsushima in 1906 and was thus of deep significance to the Japanese Navy.

Within 15 minutes the first wave of 183 aircraft was airborne, consisting of 50 high-level bombers, 40 torpedo-bombers, 51 dive-bombers and 43 fighters. This was followed shortly afterwards by the second wave which included 170 aircraft: 54 high level bombers, 81 dive-bombers, and 36 fighters. It had been planned to launch the remaining aircraft in a third wave to attack the fuel and supply depots, but after furious arguments in the Japanese High Command this did not take place, a serious mistake since the destruction of its fuel stocks would have forced the US fleet to withdraw, at least temporarily, to the West Coast. It was an error, primarily due to the ever-cautious Admiral Nagumo, for which the Japanese were to pay dearly.

The Japanese attack on Pearl Harbor represents one of the most devastating and imaginative uses of naval power in history. Most attention is usually paid to the aircraft which delivered the actual attack, but it was the carriers, lying unseen and unchallenged over the horizon, that delivered the aircraft to their take-off point and recovered them afterwards to participate in other operations elsewhere.

DUKE OF YORK

DESIGN HISTORY

The design of the King George V class was heavily constrained by political considerations, particularly the various naval agreements of the 1930s, in one of which the British and Japanese undertook not to lay down any new battleships before 1937. The British also hoped to obtain agreement at the scheduled 1936 meeting to a maximum of 14in (356mm) calibre guns for new construction. Despite this, the French and Italians (who refused to sign the London Treaty) and the Germans (who had a separate agreement with the British) had already begun the construction of fast, powerful battleships and the British were forced to follow suit.

The emphasis in the design of the new class was on heavy armament and the 14in (356mm) gun was selected, but in an unusual arrangement of two quadruple and one twin turret. This gun fired a 1,590lb (720kg) shell to a maximum range of 36,000yd (32,900m), but the mounting was complicated, not least because of the desire to eliminate the possibility of "flash," which had caused such problems at the Battle of Jutland in

BELOW: *King George V-class battleships (this is HMS* Howe) *had an unusual main armament of ten 14in (356mm) guns, which were mounted in two quadruple turrets (one forward, one aft) and one twin turret in "B" position forward.*

RIGHT: *HMS* Duke of York *which was Admiral Fraser's flagship at the Battle of North Cape. Directly engaged in the battle, the* Duke of York *showed a high standard of gunnery which eventually sank the doomed German battlecruiser,* Scharnhorst.

1916. This complexity resulted in a degree of unreliability which affected the ships in their early battles, such as that between *Prince of Wales* and *Bismarck*. These ships had excellent armour protection, the main belt being 24ft (7.5m) deep with its thickness varying from 15in (380mm) to 4.5in (115mm), while the single horizontal armoured deck was 6in (150mm) thick.

BATTLE OF NORTH CAPE: 26 DECEMBER 1943

In December 1943 HMS *Duke of York* was flagship of the Home Fleet (Admiral Fraser) and was serving as distant cover for convoy JW.55B which was on passage from Loch Ewe, Scotland to Murmansk, Russia. This convoy comprised 19 merchantmen, escorted by 15 destroyers and two corvettes, with close support from three cruisers (*Belfast, Sheffield, Norfolk*) under Rear-Admiral Burnett. *Duke of York* was accompanied by one cruiser, Jamaica, and five destroyers. The major threat was the German battlecruiser *Scharnhorst*, based in the Altenfjord in Norway, and this ship, accompanied by five destroyers, and commanded by Admiral Bey, sailed on 25 December to attack the convoy. The British, due to Ultra decryption of enemy radio signals, knew that *Scharnhorst* and its destroyers were at sea, but although Bey knew about the convoy, he was unaware of *Duke of York's* presence.

By this stage in the war British naval radar was much better than that of Germany's and when Burnett's cruisers made radar contact with *Scharnhorst* at 0920 on 26 December they were able not only to track the German ship but also to use it to bring down effective fire, in which, crucially, one round destroyed its radar antenna. *Scharnhorst* then used its superior speed to pull out of range but, despite the arrival of four destroyers from the close escort, at 1030 Burnett lost all contact with *Scharnhorst* for almost two hours. At 1220, however, *Scharnhorst* tried to break through to reach the convoy and, although the German ship got the best of the ensuing engagement, damaging both *Norfolk* and *Sheffield*, Bey then decided to return to base. This may have been because by this time he knew that an enemy battleship was in the area, but may also have been because, due to the appalling weather, he had no air cover and also because he felt the need to preserve *Scharnhorst* as Germany's last active capital ship.

Meanwhile, however, Fraser had manoeuvred *Duke of York* into a position between Bey and the Norwegian coast and because *Scharnhorst's* radar had been destroyed earlier, the first the Germans knew was at 1625 when starshells burst overhead, closely followed by shells from the British battleship. *Scharnhorst* was caught totally by surprise but recovered and soon the two big ships were slugging it out with each other. *Scharnhorst* used its speed advantage to draw away, but, paradoxically, this made matters worse since the British shells now arrived vertically against the weaker top armour rather than horizontally against the main armour belt, and in this action British gunnery, guns and ammunition all proved superior. The German ship was soon ablaze with an ever decreasing number of guns left in action, and the destroyers were then closed to launch torpedoes. *Scharnhorst* succumbed at 1930: there were just 36 survivors.

FLOWER-CLASS

DESIGN HISTORY

With war approaching in the late 1930s, the British Admiralty appreciated the threat likely to arise from German U-boats and searched for a coastal anti-submarine escort vessel which could be produced quickly, in large numbers and at reasonable cost, but which would still be effective in its primary mission, would be seaworthy, and with reasonable endurance and manoeuvrability. Other important criteria were that it had to be capable of being produced in shipyards not normally involved in naval work and suitable for handling by reservists. The requirement was stated on 2 January 1939 and Smith's Dock produced the first drawings of a design based on a lengthened version of their deep-sea trawler, *Southern Pride*, in time to be approved by 27 February. The design was then refined and the first order placed on 25 July.

The design was constantly being improved and additional equipment and longer patrols led to a need for larger crews, which meant more accommodation in an already cramped ship. This was partially solved by extending the forecastle further aft, which also made the ships more seaworthy. The ships had a reputation for "rolling on wet grass", so wider bilge keels were fitted, while increased flare and sheer above the waterline made them slightly drier. The bridge was also redesigned.

A total of 288 Flower-class corvettes were built: 164 in 17 shipyards in the United Kingdom and 124 in 13 yards in Canada. These ships served in the Royal Navy, the Royal Canadian Navy, and the United States Navy, and were also operated by crews who escaped from the occupied countries, including Belgium, France, Greece, Netherlands, Norway and Yugoslavia.

SPECIFICATIONS

COUNTRY OF ORIGIN: United Kingdom.
TYPE: corvette.
LAUNCHED: 1939–1944.
DISPLACEMENT: 1,170t standard; 1,245t full load.
DIMENSIONS: length 205.0ft (62.5m); beam 33.2ft (10.1m); draught 13.6ft (4.1m).
PROPULSION: one shaft; triple-expansion engine; two Admiralty-pattern three-drum boilers; 2,750hp; speed 16.5kt.
WEAPONS: 1 x 4in/45 BL Mk IX; 40 depth-charges.
COMPLEMENT: 85.

RIGHT: *HMS* Dianthus *rammed German submarine U-379 five times during a three-hour battle on 8 August 1942, as these scars on her bows clearly prove; just five of the U-boat's 44-man crew survived. Main gun is an elderly 4in (102mm) in a rudimentary plated turret.*

BELOW: *The redoubtable Flower-class corvettes were manned mainly by reservists and conscripts, and bore the brunt of the Battle of the Atlantic in the years 1939-1943. They were very uncomfortable but their crews were of hardy stock and outfought the U-boats.*

BATTLE OF THE ATLANTIC: 1939–1945

Flower-class corvettes fought in the Battle of the Atlantic from the first to the last days of the war. They had been designed as coastal escorts, but as shore-based aircraft pushed the U-boats further out into the Atlantic, the Flowers were forced to follow them. The defence of east-bound convoy HX.133 is typical of many engagements in which they took part. The 41 ships in the convoy sailed on 21 June and were spotted by U-203 on 21 June 1941 when 400nm due south of Greenland. Dönitz was informed and he ordered U-203 to follow and transmit beacon signals so that other U-boats could home-in to form a "wolf-pack". The British realised the threat to HX.133 and quickly assembled an escort of destroyers and Flower-class corvettes.

The first major attack came on the night of 25 June when *Gladiolus* spotted *U-71* on the surface and attacked, assisted later by *Nasturtium*. *U-71* was very seriously damaged and forced to withdraw to France. By now there were 10 escorts and 10 U-boats, and on the night 26/27 June *U-564* moved in and sank two ships (17,463t).

That night *U-556* was also moving in to attack when it was detected on sonar by *Gladiolus*, which called upon *Nasturtium* and *Celandine* for help. Cooperating closely, the three corvettes carried out a long series of attacks, in which they expended 54 depth-charges before *U-556* was forced to the surface, appearing suddenly almost underneath *Gladiolus*. The three corvettes opened fire at point-blank range with any weapon that could be brought to bear, whereupon the U-boat's commanding officer decided to scuttle. *Gladiolus* tried to board in order to save cypher documents but the boat was already sinking and the attempt had to be abandoned. Of *U-556*'s crew, 40 were rescued and five died.

Shortly after midnight on the following night *U-651* attacked and sank the commodore's ship, SS *Grayburn* (6,342t) but the U-boat was rammed and seriously damaged by the next ship in the column, SS *Anadara*. *U-651* had descended to 500ft (1,500m) when the captain decided to surface and escape under diesel power, but he was seen by the destroyer *Malcolm* which, accompanied by another destroyer, *Scimitar*, and the corvette *Nasturtium*, charged in with guns blazing. The U-boat captain decided to scuttle and all his crew were saved.

Like the Type VIIC U-boats the Flower-class design was the result of many compromises and was not ideal for its purpose. Despite this, the crews fought it hard and through dogged determination they wore their enemy down.

ILLUSTRIOUS

DESIGN HISTORY

In the late 1930s Japanese and US carriers were designed for operations in the Pacific, where the threat from land-based aircraft seemed small and they were, therefore, lightly armoured. The British, however, designed their carriers for operations in European waters where the threat was much higher and, as a result, they designed their carriers around an armoured box containing the hangar, which was intended to provide protection from horizontal fire from a 6in (152mm) shell or from air attack by a 500lb (250kg) semi-armour piercing bomb delivered from 7,000ft (2,000m). Because of limitations imposed by the various naval treaties, standard displacement could not exceed about 23,000 tons, which meant that, unlike the contemporary *Ark Royal* which had two hangars, the Illustrious class could accommodate only one hangar.

This decision to fit an armoured flightdeck proved to be of immense advantage when British carriers were operating in the Pacific in 1945 and all six suffered direct hits by *kamikazes*. US carriers were fitted with wooden flightdecks and suffered great damage and were out of action for some

SPECIFICATIONS
COUNTRY OF ORIGIN: United Kingdom.
TYPE: fleet aircraft carrier.
COMMISSIONED: 21 May 1940.
DISPLACEMENT: 23,205 tons standard; 28,619 tons full load.
DIMENSIONS: length 743.8ft (234m); beam 95.8ft (29.2m); draught 24ft (7.3m).
PROPULSION: three shafts; six Admiralty-pattern three-drum boilers; three Parson, single-reduction steam turbines; 110,100shp; speed 30.5kt.
ARMOUR: belt 4.5in (114mm); hangar side 4.5in (114mm); bulkheads 4.5-2.5in (114-64mm); flightdeck 3in (76mm).
WEAPONS: 16 x 4.5in (114mm); 48 x 2pdr; 8 x 20mm.
AIRCRAFT: 36.
COMPLEMENT: 1,500.

time, whereas the British carriers were undamaged and required only a short time before they were fully operational once again.

The class consisted of six ships, which were commissioned as follows: *Illustrious* (1940); *Formidable* (1940); *Victorious* (1941); *Indomitable* (1941); *Indefatigable* (1944) and *Implacable* (1944). Due to the limitations imposed by the hangar, the

LEFT: Illustrious *under attack by the* Luftwaffe; *hit three times, it was saved by the armoured flightdeck.*

BELOW: Illustrious, *which launched the attack on Taranto in November 1940, is seen here as it appeared during the Salerno landings, in September 1943.*

original aircraft complement was 36, but wartime pressures increased this to 54 in the first four ships and to 81 in the last two. This was achieved primarily by making use of deck parking and increasing the deck parking area by means of sponsons.

BELOW: *An Illustrious-class carrier at sea with Hurricanes warming-up on the flight-deck. The carrier is protecting one of the Malta convoys which were regularly attacked by Axis ships, submarines and aircraft, suffering great losses in men, warships and merchant ships.*

ATTACKS ON PALEMBANG: 24/29 JANUARY 1945

In January 1945 the British naval presence in the Indian Ocean comprised the Far East Fleet and the newly formed Pacific Fleet, which had been assembling and working-up in Ceylon. When it was decided to move this new fleet to Brisbane, Australia, it was arranged to carry out some operations against the Japanese en route. Thus, the fleet sailed under the designation Task Force 63 (TF.63) on 16 January 1945, comprising four Illustrious-class carriers – *Indomitable* (flag officer carriers, R Adm Vian), *Illustrious*, *Victorious* and *Indefatigable* - battleship *King George V*, four cruisers and 10 destroyers, with three submarines in support for air-sea rescue and reconnaissance.

The targets were a number of oil refineries near Palembang on the eastern end of the island of Sumatra and involved the aircraft flying over some 100 miles of Japanese-held territory to reach their targets which lay on the northern coast. The first raid took place on 24 January and consisted of 43 Grumman Avenger bombers and 12 Fairey Firefly fighter-bombers armed with rockets, with an escort of 50 fighters, a mix of Hellcats, Corsairs and Seafires. This attack was against oil refinery at Pladjoe north of Palembang and took the defenders completely by surprise. Some 20 Japanese fighters managed to take-off, of

which 14 were shot down, while another 38 aircraft were destroyed on the ground. The British lost seven aircraft due to enemy action and 25 from crash landings.

Having recovered the survivors, the British fleet hauled off to replenish and then returned for a second attack on 29 January, this time against oil refineries at Sungei Gerong, a short distance to the east of Palembang. The raid was conducted by 48 Avengers, 10 Fireflies, 24 Corsairs and 16 Hellcats. Once again the Japanese were taken by surprise, this time 30 Japanese aircraft being shot down and some 35-40 destroyed on the ground. Sixteen British aircraft did not return, although some crews were picked up by the air-sea rescue organisation. The Japanese then managed to mount an attack on the carriers by 12 bombers, but they were intercepted and every aircraft was shot down by either the fighters or the ships' anti-aircraft guns. The fleet then replenished on 30 January and sailed on to its destination in Australia.

These raids inflicted considerable damage on the oil refineries and also demonstrated to the Japanese that even in the Indonesian islands they were no longer safe from Allied action. This was made possible by the four Illustrious-class carriers.

LANDING CRAFT, TANK MARK IV

SPECIFICATIONS

COUNTRY OF ORIGIN: United Kingdom.

TYPE: landing craft.

LAUNCHED: 1942-45.

DISPLACEMENT: light 200 tons; loaded 640 tons.

DIMENSIONS: length 187.3ft (57.1m); beam 38.8ft (11.8m); draught (see text); tank hold 93.8 x 26.0ft (28.6 x 7.9m).

PROPULSION: two shafts; two Paxman diesels; 1,000hp; speed 8kt.

ARMOUR: plastic armour on steering position, compass platform, gun positions, forward winches and anchor reels.

LOAD: tanks – 6 x 40-ton (40,600kg) or 9 x 30-ton (30,500kg); trucks – 12 x 3-ton (3,100kg) loaded; general cargo – 350 tons (355,600kg).

WEAPONS: two 20mm Oerlikon.

COMPLEMENT: 12.

DESIGN HISTORY

The staff requirement for the LCT(4) was for a vessel to carry a 350-ton payload across the English Channel, deliver it over a French beach and then return to England. Earlier LCTs had too deep a draught, that of the LCT(3) being 3.5ft (1.1m) forward, 6.7ft (2.1m) aft, meaning that they beached too far from the shore. So the LCT(4) was given a greater beam and reduced weight to enable it to carry the same payload on a shallower draught – 3.1ft (0.94m) forward, 4.3ft (1.3m) aft. It was powered by two Paxman diesels driving fast-turning (1,375rpm) propellers, both turning in the same direction for ease of production, although this also made for difficult handling.

The tank hold formed a girder with heavy

LEFT: *The Landing Craft Infantry (Large) was designed to land infantry directly onto enemy beaches.*

RIGHT: *A squadron of LCT(4)s, loaded with troops and army equipment, en route to France, D-day, 6 June 1944.*

BELOW: *The LCT(4) was the most numerous vessel in the D-Day landings. It was small and simple, but without it the massive Allied armies would never have reached France.*

weights at each end: the superstructure and engines aft and the heavy winches and tank door forward. The rigidity of the whole depended upon the strength of the girder, which, in order to achieve lightness, was not great, so that, if driven into a heavy sea for too long, vibrations could be set up, resulting in a crack at the weakest point, the junction of the tank deck and the superstructure, which then split. After many mishaps this was strengthened. 864 were built of which 39 were lost.

D-DAY LANDINGS: 6 JUNE 1944

Assault Group S2" of "Naval Force S" was based at Newhaven, its D-day task being to land 185th Infantry Brigade of 3rd (British) Division in the second landing wave on Sword Beach, arriving at H+90 minutes. Assault Group S2 consisted of 12 Landing Craft Infantry (LCI) carrying three battalions of infantry, followed by 12 LCT(4)s carrying Sherman tanks, followed by 22 LCT(4)s carrying vehicles and stores, and two carrying ammunition and explosives.

Assault Group S2 received the signal to sail at noon on 5 June and sailed at 1230, heading westwards for the main transit point, officially designated "Area Z", but known to all concerned as "Piccadilly Circus". The rising sea played havoc with station-keeping but the group stayed together – which was essential in the mass of shipping – and at 0100 on 6 June passed the motor launch marking the entrance to the slow lane to Sword Beach. The lane, which had previously been cleared by minesweepers, was marked by dimly lit blue and white buoys, and the group, already under occasional fire from German shore batteries, reached the "Lowering Point", six miles off the Beach, with 20 minutes to spare. Then, at the scheduled time, it commenced its timed run-in, which required it to cover the first three miles in two columns, then to shake out into three columns, and finally, half-a-mile from the beach, to form line abreast.

During exercises that had not proved too difficult, but on D-day itself, with all the other marine traffic, sinking vessels from the first wave, Rommel's beach obstacles and artillery fire from the shore, it was more difficult, but eventually they achieved it, 30ft (9m) apart and advancing at flank speed – 14 knots. The LCTs weaved their way through the mine stakes, found a gap between vessels from the previous wave which had been unable to withdraw and then hit the beach.

Having discharged their passengers, the LCTs used their stern anchors to pull themselves off the beach and then withdrew as quickly as they could to make room for the rapidly approaching next wave. By the time the squadron had completed its task and started the return to England, two LCTs had been damaged and one, which had broken in two, was towing its front end, but all made it back to Newhaven.

The LCT(4) was the most widely used landing craft on the D-day landings and was a very small and unglamorous warship. Nevertheless, it is no exaggeration to say that without it the Allied armies would never have got to France.

AJAX, ACHILLES

SPECIFICATIONS

COUNTY OF ORIGIN: United Kingdom.

TYPE: light cruiser.

LAUNCHED: 1 March 1934.

COMMISSIONED: 12 April 1935.

DISPLACEMENT: 7,270 tons standard; 9,280 tons full load.

DIMENSIONS: Length 554.5ft (169.0m); beam 55.6ft (17.0m); draught 19.0ft (5.8m).

PROPULSION: four shafts; Parsons geared turbines; six Admiralty 3-drum boilers; 72,000shp; speed 32.5kt.

ARMOUR: magazines 3.5in (90mm); belt 3in (76mm); bulkheads 1.5in (38mm).

WEAPONS: 8 x 6in (152mm) (4 x 2); 4 x 4in (102mm) (4 x 1).

TORPEDO TUBES: 8 x 21in (533mm) torpedo tubes.

AIRCRAFT: two Seafox floatplanes.

COMPLEMENT: 570.

DESIGN HISTORY

The five Leander-class ships were completed in 1933-34, the only single-stack cruisers to be built for the Royal Navy in the 20th Century. They were armed with eight 6in (152mm) guns in four twin turrets and eight 21in (533mm) torpedo tubes, and had a degree of armoured protection, with a 3in (76mm) belt which covered the machinery spaces. Like most inter-war British cruisers they were equipped with a catapult, and carried two Seafox floatplanes, which were used for reconnaissance, spotting fall of shot and warning of incoming torpedoes.

RIGHT: *British Leander-class cruiser, HMS* Achilles. *The single funnel and general appearance led Captain Langsdorff and his well-trained bridge crew to mistake these two cruisers for destroyers. As a result, Langsdorff committed his ship to battle with the British force .*

BATTLE OF THE RIVER PLATE: 13 DECEMBER 1939

The German armoured cruiser *Admiral Graf Spee* (Captain Langsdorff) operated in the South Atlantic and Indian Ocean from September to December 1939, causing the British considerable problems. Some 34 British and French warships deployed specifically to search for the raider, one such group, commanded by Commodore Harwood, consisting of four cruisers: two light, *Ajax* and *Achilles*, and two heavy, *Cumberland* and *Exeter*. Harwood's task was to protect British shipping off the Atlantic coast of South America and he assessed that Langsdorff must eventually attack shipping off the River Plate. He was right and was patrolling there with *Ajax*, *Achilles* and *Exeter* (*Cumberland* was in the Falkland Islands) when *Graf Spee* arrived at dawn on 13 December.

The Germans spotted the British first, but made a crucial error in identifying the two single-funnel Leanders as destroyers; by the time Langsdorff had realised his mistake, the British had seen *Graf Spee* and a battle was inevitable. Harwood headed for the enemy, with *Exeter* forming one division, *Ajax* and *Achilles* the other. *Graf Spee's* 11in (280mm) guns were much more powerful and longer ranged than *Exeter's* 8in (203mm) guns, but he German guns were in two triple turrets, making ranging and engaging multiple targets much more difficult.

Forced to concentrate on one target, Langsdorff selected *Exeter*, and *Graf Spee* was soon scoring hits. The eighth salvo knocked out *Exeter's* "B" turret, killing many of those on the bridge, and forcing the wounded captain to move to the emergency control position aft. *Exeter* also scored hits, some

penetrating the armoured belt, much to the German's surprise. Harwood, seeing *Exeter* so badly damaged, brought the two light cruisers closer to *Graf Spee*, forcing Langsdorff to shift his fire, thus giving *Exeter* a respite. Handling the two cruisers like destroyers, Harwood scored repeated hits, although the 6in (152mm) shells did comparatively little damage, while several torpedoes failed to hit the target.

At 0725 *Ajax* suffered a hit which put both X and Y turrets out of action and caused a number of casualties. Thus, by this time, *Exeter* was out of the action, having suffered 61 casualties and a great deal of damage, *Ajax* was damaged but battleworthy, while *Achilles* was unscathed. To the surprise of the British Langsdorff made for the River Plate, entering Montevideo harbour at 2350 that night. *Ajax* and *Achilles* stood off the river mouth, watching *Graf Spee*, but *Exeter* departed for the Falkland Islands. Langsdorff was able to spend only a few days in the neutral port of Montevideo before being forced to leave. He blew his ship up outside territorial waters and took his crew to Buones Aires, where he committed suicide two days later.

Nobody doubts Langsdorff's courage or integrity, but some of his decisions during this day are hard to understand. It would have made sense for him to have finished off *Exeter* but he did not do so, while in heading for Montevideo he put himself into a trap from which there was no escape. *Exeter* acquitted itself well, having taken the brunt of the punishment suffered by the British ships and inflicting most of the damage on *Graf Spee*, but *Ajax's* and *Achilles'* speed and manoeuverability compensated for the lack of power of their 6in guns.

ABOVE: Graf Spee *lies burning in the River Plate, a major blow to German prestige and the start of Hitler's disenchantment with his navy. Langsdorff calculated that his ship was bound to be defeated by the British and French navies and decided that the heavy loss of life was not worth it; he paid with his own life.*

LEFT: *Following the German defeat, HMS* Achilles *pays a courtesy visit to Buenos Aires in January 1940. Because of the rules governing neutral ports, the ship was able to remain for only 48 hours. Note the 6in (152mm) guns, which were not as powerful as the 11in (280mm) guns in* Graf Spee, *but the British ships were fast and manoeuvrable.*

ONSLOW

DESIGN HISTORY

Among the most handsome warships ever built, British World War II single-stack destroyers combined smooth lines with a dashing and businesslike air. The sixteen-strong O/P classes were a slightly smaller, more utilitarian version of the design, with HMS *Onslow*, leader of the O-class, being launched at John Brown's Clydebank yard on 31 March 1941. Most ships in the class were armed with 4in (102mm) guns, but *Onslow* was one of four mounting the heavier and more effective 4.7in (120mm) gun – two forward, two aft. There was a quadruple 21in (533mm) torpedo tube mounted in the waist, and anti-aircraft armament comprised a 4in high-angle gun and a quadruple 2-pounder "pom-pom".

SPECIFICATIONS

COUNTRY OF ORIGIN: Great Britain.
TYPE: destroyer.
LAUNCHED: 31 March 1941.
DISPLACEMENT: 1,550 tons standard; 2,270 tons deep load.
DIMENSIONS: length 328.7ft (100.2m); beam 35.0ft (10.7m); draught 13.5ft (4.1m).
PROPULSION: two Admiralty 3-drum boilers; 2 Parson steam turbines; 40,000shp; 37kt.
WEAPONS: 4 x 4.7in (120mm) (4 x 1); 1 x 4in (102mm) high-angle; 4 x 2-pdr pom-pom; (1 x 4); 4 x 21in (533mm) (1 x 4) torpedo tubes.
COMPLEMENT: 212.

ABOVE LEFT: *Onslow after its epic battle. The splinter holes in the funnel and bridge and numerous steam leaks are evidence of the ordeal the ship and crew went through.*

LEFT: *Sailors aboard the destroyer depot ship cheer as HMS* Onslow *returns from its epic battle. The ship suffered some 40 casualties when hit by a salvo from the German heavy cruiser,* Hipper.

RIGHT: *British World War II destroyers were handsome and dashing ships, as shown here by HMS* Onslow.

BATTLE OF THE BARENTS SEA: 31 DECEMBER 1942

The Arctic convoys sailed parallel to the coast of German-occupied Norway, rendering them vulnerable to interception by enemy warships, U-boats and aircraft. One such convoy, JW.51, was divided into two, the first part, JW.51A, consisting of 16 merchantmen, leaving Loch Ewe in northern Scotland on 15 December, escorted by seven destroyers, two corvettes, one minesweeper and two trawlers, with a close escort of two cruisers (*Sheffield, Jamaica*) and two destroyers, and distant cover from the Home Fleet. The convoy arrived undetected off Murmansk on 25 December, although five merchantmen were then sunk by a combination of German air attacks and mines.

The second half, JW.51B, sailed on 22 December consisting of 14 merchantmen. The escort, commanded by Captain Robert Sherbrooke, consisted of seven destroyers (*Onslow, Oribi, Obedient, Orwell, Achates, Bulldog*), two corvettes, a minesweeper and two trawlers. The close escort was to be provided by *Sheffield* and *Jamaica,* returning from Murmansk for the purpose, with distant cover of a heavy cruiser and three destroyers and, once again, support from the Home Fleet, if needed.

JW.51B was detected on 24 December and on 29 December a strong German force put to sea. The commander, Vice-Admiral Kummetz, split his force, with the heavy cruiser, *Admiral Hipper* and three destroyers approaching the convoy from the north, while the armoured cruiser, *Lützow,* also accompanied by three destroyers, would come from the south. *Obdurate* sighted an approaching German destroyer at 0830 on 31 December and an hour later *Onslow*'s lookouts glimpsed the cruiser *Hipper* through the gloom. Sherbrooke immediately headed for this much heavier ship, but signalled as he did so for support from the close escort cruisers.

Onslow and *Orwell* held *Hipper* at bay for nearly two hours, using smoke and snow showers to cover their approaches, as they harried the German cruiser. At about 1020, however, a salvo from *Hipper* hit *Onslow* forward, both forward turrets being destroyed and causing some 40 casualties, including on the bridge, where Sherbrooke was hit in the face and stood with his left eye dangling out of its socket. He insisted on continuing to direct his ship until another destroyer had assumed command of the escort, when *Onslow*, damaged but unbeaten, took station at the head of the convoy, while three other destroyers held *Hipper* at bay.

Kummetz worked his way round to the head of the convoy and suddenly reappeared at about 1100, when rounds from *Hipper* battered the destroyer *Achates,* causing heavy casualties. *Obdurate* and *Obedient* were also hit, but at this point *Hipper*'s captain became concerned about the dangers of torpedo attack and turned away, only to find himself under fire from the approaching cruisers, *Jamaica* and *Sheffield*, arriving in answer to Sherbrooke's earlier appeal.

The German commander had received a signal from naval high command telling him that he was to ". . . exercise restraint if you contact enemy of comparable strength, since it is undesirable to run excessive risks to the cruisers . . ." and he disengaged, but not before *Sheffield* had found and sunk the destroyer *Friedrich Eckholdt.* Despite the atrocious weather, the British destroyers were skilfully used against a much more powerful enemy and Sherbrooke was awarded the Victoria Cross for this epic defence against heavy odds.

RIGHT: *Captain R StV Sherbrook, DSO (seen here as a commander), was awarded the Victoria Cross for his epic defence of Convoy JW.51B on 31 December 1942.*

X-CRAFT

SPECIFICATIONS

COUNRY OF ORIGIN: United Kingdom.
TYPE: miniature submarine.
LAUNCHED: 1942-45.
DISPLACEMENT: surface 26.9 tons; submerged 29.7 tons.
DIMENSIONS: length 51.6ft (15.7m); beam (less side charges) 7.3ft (2.2m).
PROPULSION: single shaft; Gardner diesel, 42bhp; electric motor, 30shp; 6.6kt surface, speed 5.5kt submerged.
MAX DEPTH: 300ft (91m).
WEAPONS: two side charges, each 2 tons high explosive.
COMPLEMENT: 3 (later 4).

DESIGN HISTORY

The design of the X-craft was based on that of a small submarine developed in the mid-1930s for riverine use. They were simply very small submarines, with a crew of three (later increased to four), with two detachable sidetanks, each containing two tons of high explosive and detonated by a clockwork fuze which was set from inside the craft immediately prior to release. Because of its limited range and seakeeping ability, an X-craft, manned by a passage crew, was towed to the vicinity of the target by a larger, conventional submarine. The normal arrangement was that the larger submarine travelled on the surface with the X-craft submerged at a depth of 50ft (15m) for as long as possible, but then both travelled submerged for the final approach to the release area. There, both surfaced and the operational crew took over. At least one larger submarine would later return to a rendezvous to recover crews returning from the attack.

ABOVE: *British X-craft had two four-man crews. One, the "passage crew", manned them during the voyage to the operational area, when they were towed by larger submarines. The second crew then took over for the operation itself.*

RIGHT: *An officer emerges from X-25. The explosive was in two sidetanks which were detached beneath the target, following which the craft escaped, taking the crew to a rendezvous with a waiting submarine and the voyage back to base.*

ATTACK ON *TIRPITZ*: 22 SEPTEMBER 1943

The German battleship *Tirpitz* deployed to Norwegian waters in 1942 from where it posed a permanent threat to the Allied Arctic convoys to and from Russia and it was also possible that it might break-out into the Atlantic. Sheltering in a fjord, *Tirpitz* was difficult to attack, but the X-craft miniature submarines offered a solution, and Operation Source was mounted in late 1943. This involved six of the 4-man submarines, with three separate targets: *X-5, X-6* and *X-7* were to attack *Tirpitz* in the Kaafjord; while *X-9* and *X-10* were to attack battlecruiser *Scharnhorst* and *X-8 the* heavy cruiser *Lützow*, both in Langefjord.

The attack force sailed on 11/12 September, the X-craft being towed to their operational area by six larger submarines. Two craft were lost in transit: *X-8* had to be scuttled and *X-9* was lost after the tow parted. The remaining four boats arrived at the release point on 20 September, the passage crews having suffered eight days of acute discomfort and danger, and the operational crews then took over. They slipped their tows, as planned, off Soroy Island, but *X-10* was forced to spend three days trying to repair a variety of faults. Eventually the captain returned to the rendezvous, where his crew was recovered by the "mother ship". In fact, both *Scharnhorst* and *Lützow* were at sea on gunnery trials on the day of the attack, so the misadventures which befell these three X-craft did not prejudice the main operation.

X-6 suffered a series of mishaps: the periscope flooded; a sidecharge sprang a leak; the periscope motor burst into flames from a short-circuit; it hit a rock just short of the target;, and then hit another obstruction underneath the target. Despite all this, Lieutenant Cameron, its commander, managed to drop the charges in the correct position, but then, escape being impossible, he surfaced and surrendered.

X-7 also reached the target and dropped both charges correctly and was making its escape when the charges underneath *Tirpitz* blew up, the shock wave forcing the craft to the surface. The captain, Lieutenant Place, and one other crew member survived, but the two others died. *X-5* appears to have laid its charges under *Tirpitz* and surfaced briefly after the explosion, but was never seen again.

The damage to *Tirpitz* was serious, with a hole in its bottom, considerable buckling, two turrets lifted off their roller tracks, one rudder and one propeller damaged, and most radio and radar antennas damaged beyond repair, all of which took six months to repair. This was a major achievement for such small craft, at the cost of nine men killed and six captured. The materiel loss of all six X-craft was a small price to pay.

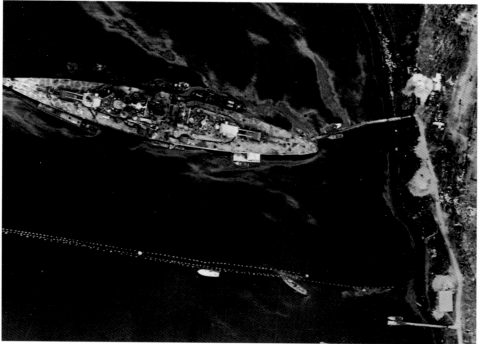

ABOVE: *X-Craft, X-25, with the commanding officer standing in the pulpit – there was no conning tower in such small submarines. In addition to the attack on* Tirpitz, *the Japanese cruiser* Takao *was sunk in Singapore harbour by XE-3 on 31 July 1945.*

LEFT: *German battleship* Tirpitz *in Kaafjord, Norway, in July 1944. Note the anti-torpedo nets and the small boats around the battleship, which are carrying out repairs.*

ESSEX CLASS

DESIGN HISTORY

These aircraft carriers were enlarged versions of the three-ship Yorktown-class which had been constructed in the 1930s and were, therefore, constrained in several respects by the London and Washington Naval treaties. The Essex-class, however, was free of all such restrictions. Thus, they were longer, had greater displacement and were better armed, although the aircraft accommodation was virtually the same: Yorktown-class – 96, Essex-class – 91. The Essex-class also had a new upper armour deck 1in (38mm) thick, at the hangar deck level, which was intended to explode armour piercing shells before they hit the main armour deck protecting the machinery and fuel tanks below; unlike the British contemporary, the Illustrious-class, the Essex-class did not have an armoured flight deck.

They had a long, clear flightdeck with the combined island/stack to starboard. The original plan was for three catapults, two on the forward flightdeck and one in the hangar launching athwartships, although quite what purpose the latter was intended to serve is unclear and it was eliminated before the first-of-class was completed. The ships had two elevators centrally in the flightdeck and a third, deck-edge elevator forward of the island on the starboard side. They had a formidable AA armament, which was just as well since these carriers were prime targets for the Japanese air attacks in 1944/45. Twelve of the class were damaged in air attacks, but although they suffered many casualties and lost a large number of aircraft, none was sunk.

The original air wing comprised 90 aircraft (36 fighters, 36 reconnaissance/bombers, 18 torpedo-bombers), but by the war's end this had increased to 103 (73 fighters, 15 bombers and 15 torpedo-bombers).

ABOVE: USS Essex, first of the new class of large carriers. One novel feature in this class was the side elevator, which was intended to speed up the transfer of aircraft between flightdeck and hangar. Efficient and popular, it has been fitted in all subsequent US carriers.

BELOW: The hangar of an Essex-class carrier, USS Intrepid (CV-11) following a hit by a kamikaze on its unarmoured flightdeck.

RIGHT: *A fighter comes aboard an Essex-class carrier bristling with armament.*

BELOW: *Crewmen aboard USS* Bunker Hill *(CV-17) fight fires caused by* kamikaze *attacks off Okinawa, 11 May 1945.*

RIGHT: *The Essex-class carrier* Hornet *fires its 40mm guns as its aircraft carry out strikes on Tokyo, 16 February 1945.*

BELOW: *Essex-class carrier, USS* Bunker Hill *(CV-7), survives two near-misses on its port quarter, while the Japanese bomber, its tail shot off by the defending AA guns begins its final dive into the sea.*

BATTLE OF THE PHILIPPINE SEA: 19–21 JUNE 1944.

Essex class carriers took part in numerous battles in the Pacific, one of the most notable being the Battle of the Philippine Sea, in which fifteen carriers took part, six of them Essex-class: *Bunker Hill*, *Essex*, *Hornet*, *Lexington*, *Wasp* and *Yorktown*. The US assault on Saipan, commanded by Admiral Spruance, began on 15 June 1944 and appeared to offer the Japanese fleet, commanded by Admiral Ozawa, an opportunity to impose a smashing defeat on the US fleet.

Ozawa launched his first air attack on the morning of 19 June, despatching 372 aircraft in four waves between 0800 and 1100, but the approaching aircraft were detected by US radar. This enabled 300 US fighters to be launched at the critical moment, which proceeded to shoot down 242 enemy aircraft in the "Great Marianas Turkey Shoot", at the cost of 29 US fighters lost and one bomb hit on the battleship *South Dakota*. A further 30 Japanese aircraft were shot down when they tried to reach the airfields at Guam. Meanwhile, US submarines had penetrated

Ozawa's fleet and sank the carriers *Taiho* and *Shokaku*.

Thus, the first phase ended with the Japanese having lost two carriers and 346 aircraft for negligible losses on the US side. Ozawa started to withdraw but was delayed by the need to replenish some of his ships and the US fleet was within air range on 20 June, enabling it to launch a massive attack by 216 aircraft. The few Japanese aircraft remaining tried to defend their fleet but were massively outnumbered and the US aircraft sank another carrier and two tankers, and destroyed a further 65 aircraft, leaving Ozawa with 35 aircraft from the 473 he had started with the previous morning.

The US lost 20 aircraft over the Japanese fleet but darkness fell as the remainder returned to their own fleet and despite the US ships making lights to serve as beacons 80 aircraft were forced to ditch, although determined rescue efforts reduced the men lost to 42. It was a remarkable victory for the US fleet and was almost entirely due to the carriers and their aircraft.

LEFT: *A Japanese bomber, already on fire, heads for Essex (CV-9), 25 November 1944, in one of many direct attacks as the Japanese desperately tried to halt the advance of the US carriers.*

BELOW: *A Japanese aircraft dives in flames over a US carrier in the battle for the Marianas. US carriers were the main targets for such desperate Japanese attacks. In the foreground are two Grumman TBM Avengers.*

FLETCHER CLASS

DESIGN HISTORY

At the end of World War I the US Navy found itself with a .plethora of flush-deck destroyers and, not surprisingly, no new class was built until the Farragut class of 1932, which had superimposed guns in B and X positions and an enclosed bridge. Ten more classes then followed with a number of minor differences between each until the first of the Fletcher class – arguably the finest all-round destroyers of the war – was launched on 3 May 1942.

There were a number of significant differences from their immediate predecessors, the Benson-

SPECIFICATIONS
COUNTRY OF ORIGIN: United States of America.
TYPE: destroyer.
COMMISSIONED: 1942–1945.
DISPLACEMENT: 2,050 tons standard; 2,940 tons full load.
DIMENSIONS: length 376ft (114.6m); beam 39.3ft (12m); draught 17.8ft (5.4m).
PROPULSION: two shafts; four Babcok & Wheeler or Foster-Wheeler boilers; two GE/Westinghouse geared turbines; 60,000shp; speed 37kt.
WEAPONS: 5 x 5in (127mm) (1 x 5); 4 x 1.1in (28mm); 2–10 x 40mm; 4–11 x 20mm; 10 x 21in (533mm) (2 x 5) torpedo bombs.
COMPLEMENT: 273.

RIGHT: *A direct result of the Japanese air attacks was the hasty addition of AA guns to all types of US warships. Here the quarterdeck of a Fletcher-class destroyer has three extra 20mm guns.*

BELOW: *A Fletcher-class fleet destroyer passes an Essex-class carrier off Okinawa, 1 April 1945.*

RIGHT: *A Fletcher-class destroyer battles against the waves during a Pacific storm. Reckoned by experts to be one of the finest destroyer designs of World War II, the Fletchers fought hard throughout the war, not least at the Battle of Savo Island on 13 November 1942.*

class. Most noticeable were that they reverted to a flush-deck design and were some 30ft (9.2m) longer, but they also had a very significant increase in full load displacement from 2,395 tons to 2,924 tons. Main armament was five 5in (127mm) guns in single turrets and 10 21in (533mm) torpedo tubes, while the anti-aircraft battery started with four 1.1in (28mm) and four 20mm, but by the end of the war was five twin 40mm and seven 20mm. Another difference was that previous classes had single-reduction turbines but these were changed in the Fletchers to double-reduction turbines.

BATTLE OF SAVO ISLAND: 13 NOVEMBER 1942

As in all navies the US Navy employed its destroyers on a wide variety of tasks, such as convoy escorts and in ASW hunting groups, but they also frequently became involved in major fleet actions, serving alongside battleships or cruisers. One of the first such actions in which Fletcher-class ships took part was the First Naval Battle of Guadalcanal (12–13 November 1942).

The Japanese force involved was the 11th Battleship Squadron, commanded by Vice-Admiral Abe, whose mission was to bombard US forces ashore at Henderson Field on Guadalcanal. Abe deployed his force with two destroyers as advance guard, followed by three lines of ships: the centre line consisted of the light cruiser *Nagara*, followed by the battleships *Hiyaei* and *Kirishima*; with the escorting destroyers in two lines, three to port and six to starboard.

This force had been detected by US air reconnaissance and TG.76.4, commanded by Rear-Admiral Callaghan, was hastily redeployed to meet it. Callaghan had five cruisers under command – *Atlanta, Helena, Juneau, Portland* and *San Francisco*, and eight destroyers, five of the Benham/Benson classes – *Barton, Laffey, Monsenn, Sterett* and *Aaron Ward* – and three of the very latest Fletcher-class – *Cushing, Fletcher* and *O'Bannon*.

Abe took his force southwards down the passage between Savo Island to the north and Guadalcanal to the south on the moonless night of 13 November 1942 as Callaghan's TG.76.4 advanced northwards to meet him. The Japanese did not have radar, while the only US ship to be fitted was *Helena*, which was not the flagship. Thus, the first the two groups knew was when the American ships found themselves actually passing between the lines of Japanese ships. The Japanese were the first to respond and *Atlanta* was sunk by a mixture of gunfire from *Hiyei* and torpedoes from destroyers.

It was a most confusing battle fought at very close quarters, with ships passing as close as 3-400 yards (275–365m) from each other. The destroyers *Cushing* and *Laffey* engaged the battleship *Hiyeai* and were both sunk, but the cumulative effect of more than 50 hits on the Japanese ship left it circling with a defective rudder and it was finished off by two air-delivered torpedoes the following morning.

In the confusion several "blue-on-blue" engagements took place and at one point Admiral Callaghan realised that *San Francisco* was firing at the burning *Atlanta* and ordered a brief ceasefire, but unfortunately this enabled *Kirishima* to engage *San Francisco*, killing Callaghan. The destroyers *Barton* and *Monsenn* were both hit by Japanese torpedoes and sunk.

By the end of this epic engagement the US had lost two cruisers and four destroyers and all the surviving ships were damaged except for the cruiser *Helena* and destroyer *Fletcher*. The Japanese had lost one battleship and two destroyers, but they failed to shell Henderson Field and withdrew, leaving the United States the undoubted victors, an achievement in which the three new Fletcher-class destroyers had played a major role.

GATO-CLASS

SPECIFICATIONS

COUNTRY OF ORIGIN: United States of America.
TYPE: fleet submarine.
COMMISSIONED: 1941–1945.
DISPLACEMENT: 1,526 tons standard; 2,410 tons submerged.
DIMENSIONS: length 311.8ft (95.0m); beam 27.2ft (8.3m), draught 15.3ft (4.7m).
PROPULSION: two shafts; two diesel engines, 5,400 shp; two electric motors, 2,740shp; speed surfaced 20.3kt, submerged 8.8kt.
WEAPONS: 1 x 3in (76mm); 2 x 0.50in MG; 2 x 0.30in MG; torpedo tubes 10 x 21in (533mm) (six bow, four stern); 24 torpedoes or 40 mines.
COMPLEMENT: 80.

DESIGN HISTORY

The 73 submarines of the Gato-class were the "fleet boats" which, together with the later, and almost identical Balao-class, bore the brunt of the US unrestricted submarine campaign in the Pacific. The Gato design was a progressive development of the six-boat Tambor-class, being 4ft (1.22m) longer and with 350 tons greater displacement, most of which was used to install better diesels and a greater number of battery cells to give improved range and performance, both surfaced and submerged. Water bunkerage, a vital factor on trans-Pacific patrols, was also increased.

The original concept was for a submarine which

LEFT: *USS* Barb *(SS-220) standing out to sea in "as built" condition, with an overall black paint scheme and no hull number displayed. Built by the Electric Boat Co at Groton, Connecticut, it was launched on 2 April 1942 and commissioned on 8 July 1942; it survived the war.*

LEFT: Robalo *(SS-273) is launched at Manitowoc, Wisconsin. Deep inland, the yard built 28 boats, the fastest in 9¹/₂ months, which then took six days to reach the sea by river and canal.*

BELOW: *The internal arrangement of USS* Barb *(SS-220). US submarines were much larger than Type VIIs, as they were designed for lengthy patrols over vast distances in the Pacific. Note the torpedo tubes: six forward and four aft.*

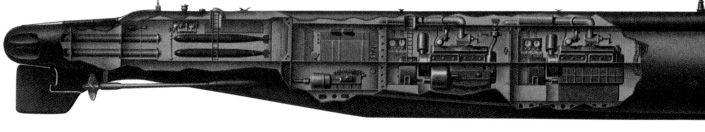

could operate with a surface fleet (hence their classification as "fleet boats") which was why they had such a high surface speed (20.25 knots), but in the event they never operated in such a way, and their speed and range were used instead to enable them to reach distant patrol areas more rapidly.

They had six bow torpedo tubes, and a

particularly heavy stern battery of four tubes. Twenty-four torpedoes were carried; a large number, but necessary for the long patrols. The Gatos were followed by the Balao-class which differed only in being constructed of stronger steel, increasing diving depth to 400ft (122m). Of the 132 Balaos ordered, 101 saw war service.

PACIFIC CAMPAIGN: 1941–1945

A small number of the early Gatos operated in the Atlantic and Mediterranean for a short period in 1943, during which *Herring* sank The German *U-136* in the Bay Of Biscay, but another, *Dorado*, was lost in the Atlantic. Otherwise the Gatos were employed entirely in the Pacific where their main task was to attack enemy shipping, although they were also used to lay mines, run supplies to guerrillas, reconnoitre landing beaches, pick up downed US aircrew and even carry out shore bombardments.

Their highest priority targets were Japanese warships, followed by merchant ships, and these boats were supremely successful in attacking both. The highest scoring "ace" was Commander Richard O'Kane who sank 24 ships (93,824 tons) while the highest scoring boat against Japanese merchant shipping was *Flasher* which sank 100,213 tons: *Barb* (SS-220), *Rasher* and *Silversides* were close behind with more than 90,000 tons each. Several Congressional Medals of Honor were won by captains of these boats, including Commander Eugene Fluckey of *Barb* and Commander O'Kane of *Tang*.

US submarines accounted for 1,314 Japanese vessels, a total of 5.3 million tons, but an even more telling statistic is the proportional responsibility for Japanese shipping losses inflicted by US forces: submarines – 57 per cent; aircraft – 33 per cent;

surface ships and mines – 10 per cent. US submarines sank seven Japanese aircraft carriers, including *Shinano*, the largest carrier to serve in any navy in World War II.

The Gato-class consisted of 73 boats of which 57 survived the war. Sixteen were lost, 11 due to enemy action; one was sunk in error by friendly forces; three were lost in accidents; and one disappeared, "cause unknown". These boats were large and provided considerably more space for their crews than contemporary British or German submarines, which was necessary in view of their long trans-Pacific patrols. Their speed enabled them to manoeuvre rapidly to take up good torpedo launching positions. Another advantage was that they were of all-welded construction, which not only made for a more robust hull, but also made them easier to construct, being built at four yards: Electric Boat, Groton; Portsmouth and Mare Island Navy Yards; and Manitowoc, Wisconsin, which was over 1,000 miles from the open sea.

The major operational problem they suffered from was not actually due to the boats themselves, but the unreliability of the torpedoes and triggers in the period from 1941 to early 1943, which resulted in many lost opportunities. Overall, however, the victory achieved by these excellent boats was one of the outstanding achievements of World War II.

RIGHT: *Highest scoring boat was* Flasher *with 100,213 tons. This is IJN destroyer* Yamakaze, *torpedoed and sunk by USS* Nautilus *on 25 June 1945.*

IOWA CLASS

SPECIFICATIONS

COUNTRY OF ORIGIN: United States of America.

TYPE: battleship.

LAUNCHED: 1942–44.

COMMISSIONED: 1943-44.

DISPLACEMENT: 48,110 tons standard; 57,540 tons full load.

DIMENSIONS: length 887.3ft (270m); beam 108.1ft (33.0m); draught 36.3ft (11.0m).

PROPULSION: four shafts; General Electric geared steam turbines; 8 Babcock & Wilcox boilers; 200,000shp; speed 32.5kt.

ARMOUR: belt 12.3in (310mm); decks 1.5in + 4.7in + 5.5in (38+120+140mm); turrets 19.7in–7.3in (495–185mm).

WEAPONS: 9 x 16in (406mm); 20 x 5in (127mm) DP; 60/80 x 40mm AA; 49-60 20mm AA.

AIRCRAFT: three.

COMPLEMENT: 1,921.

DESIGN HISTORY

The requirement for the Iowa-class of fast battleships arose in response to two threats posed by the expanding Japanese Navy. The first was the rumour which emerged from Japan in the late 1930s of the construction of 46,000 ton fast battleships, which, as events were to prove, was quite correct except that it underestimated the size of the new ships by no less than 35 per cent. Second was the fear that the Japanese were planning to form fast carrier task groups, escorted by fast cruisers or Kongo-class battlecruisers; again, as Pearl Harbor was to show, this was correct.

These two factors led the United States Navy to design a new class of fast battleship of its own, even though the high speed requirement necessitated a very long hull and great power. The protection system was generally similar to that of the preceding South Dakota class except that the belt was no longer sloped internally, but was attached directly to the inside of the hull plating, as opposed to outside where it would have added to the hydrodynamic drag. Four longitudinal torpedo bulkheads were placed inside the tapered belt and a remarkable feature of the class was the provision of two heavily armoured decks with a splinter deck between them. These two armoured decks had a combined thickness of about 12in (305mm) giving the ships unparalleled protection against plunging shells and bombs. The ships were armed with nine 16in (406mm) guns in three triple turrets, but had a particularly heavy anti-aircraft armament consisting of 20 5in (127mm) dual-purpose guns, 80 40mm and some 50 20mm.

ABOVE LEFT: Missouri.
*Note secondary armament
of 20 5in (127mm) guns
around the superstructure.*

LEFT: *By 1943, the carrier
was predominant; as a result
the main tasks for battleships
were shore bombardment (as
here) or close AA defence.*

Bombardment of Muroran: 15 July 1945

The class consisted of four ships – *Iowa*, *New Jersey*, *Missouri* and *Wisconsin* – commissioned in 1943 (first two) and 1944 (last two), and all joined the Pacific Fleet. Since by then there were very few Japanese surface warships left, however, they served principally as carrier escorts, where their very heavy anti-aircraft armament proved of great value, especially when dealing with *kamikaze* attacks.

As the inexorable advance continued, however, the US Navy ran out of targets as the Japanese Navy had virtually ceased to exist. As a result, the battleships were used for fire support missions against shore targets, one such mission taking place in July 1945, when Task Force 38 (TF.38) sailed from Leyte Gulf for operations against mainland Japan. This huge force carried out air attacks on Tokyo on 10 July and then split up for a series of independent attacks on shore targets. One of these attacks was conducted by Task Force 34.1 (TF.34.1) commanded by Rear-Admiral Badger, and comprising battleships *Iowa*, *Missouri* and *Wisconsin*, cruisers *Atlanta* and *Dayton*, seven destroyers of Desron 54 and the radar picket *Frank Knox* with the fleet commander, Admiral Halsey "along for the ride".

On 14 July TF.34.1 bombarded the town of Kamaishi on Honshu, some 250 miles (400km) north of Tokyo and then carried on northwards to the island of Hokkaido, where, on 15 July, it attacked targets in Muroran, an industrial town at the southern end of the island of Hokkaido. This involved a daylight approach, steaming well into a large bay, landlocked on three sides, which caused some slight apprehension aboard the ships, but it was a measure of US naval supremacy that they did so without any challenge from Japanese forces by sea, air or land, although all crews remained on anti-aircraft alert throughout the operation.

The approach took three hours and the bombardment started at 0936 at a range of 31,800yd (18 miles/39km) , and lasted for an hour, during which time 860 16in shells were fired. The targets were the Wanishi Ironworks (which produced pig iron and coke) and the Nihon Steel Company. The bombardment had a devastating effect, the only serious difficulty encountered being that the detonation of the high-explosive shells kicked up such an enormous amount of smoke and dust that it was virtually impossible to spot the fall of shot accurately.

The prospect of battleship versus battleship engagements had disappeared in 1944, never to return, but this shore bombardment role continued for the few remaining weeks of the war and was to assume increasing importance in later conflicts in Korea, Indochina and the Mediterranean. It proved to be a role for which these powerful United States battleships were uniquely suited.

ABOVE: New Jersey (BB-62) and Essex-class carrier Hancock (CV-19) cope with a typhoon off the Philippines on 18-19 December 1944.

BELOW: USS Missouri. With nine 16in (406mm) guns, powerful anti-aircraft battery, speed of 32.5 knots and excellent protection, the four Iowas were the finest battleships ever built. They were also greatly loved in the USA, remaining in service until the 1990s.

WASHINGTON

SPECIFICATIONS
COUNTRY OF ORIGIN: United States of America.
TYPE: battleship.
COMMISSIONED: 15 May 1941.
DISPLACEMENT: 36,600 tons standard; 44,800 tons full load.
DIMENSIONS: length 729ft (222.6m); beam 108ft (33m); draught 35ft (10.5m).
PROPULSION: four shafts; eight Babcock & Wilcox boilers; four GE geared-turbines; 121,000shp; speed 28kt.
ARMOUR: belt 12-6.6in; armoured deck 5.5-5in.
WEAPONS: 9 x 16in (406mm) (3 x 3); 20 x 5in (127mm) (10 x 2); 16 x 1.1in (28mm) (4 x 4); 12 x 0.50in (12.7mm) (12 x 1).
AIRCRAFT: three.
COMPLEMENT: 2,339.

DESIGN HISTORY

The two ships of the North Carolina-class – *North Carolina* and *Washington* – were approved in June 1936, but the production order was not placed until August 1937, making them the first US battleships to be built after the lifting of the Washington Naval Treaty limitations. They were originally to have been armed with three quadruple 14in (356mm) turrets but with the end of the treaty limitations this was changed to nine 16in (408mm) guns in three triple turrets, although these heavier weapons entailed a 2kt reduction in maximum speed. Their protection,

however, was designed to withstand attack by 14in (356mm) shells which proved adequate in service.

Previous classes of US battleships had been powered by turbo-electric drive, but these two ships were fitted with geared turbines, which proved to be very troublesome initially and needed a great deal of maintenance. In fact, although they were designated "fast" battleships their maximum speed was only 28

knots, partly due to the heavier guns, but also due to the great range needed for Pacific operations, in this case 17,450nm at 15kt. Despite these shortcomings, these ships had the best anti-aircraft defences of any contemporary battleship, had an excellent turning circle and their wide beam gave them good underwater protection and made them a stable gun platform.

SECOND BATTLE OF GUADALCANAL: 15 NOVEMBER 1942.

*W*ashington had a unique achievement in that it was the only US battleship to sink an enemy battleship during the whole of World War II. Its victim was the Japanese Kongo-class battleship *Kirishima*, which, although it had been launched as a battlecruiser in 1913, had been thoroughly modernised in the 1930s and was a very effective warship with a main armament of eight 14in (356mm) guns, a new armour belt and new engines giving it a speed of 30 knots.

On 13 November 1942, following the first battle of Guadalcanal, Admiral Halsey ordered Task Force 64 (Rear-Admiral Lee) to protect the island from an anticipated Japanese attack. TF.64 comprised two modern battleships, *Washington* (flag) and *South Dakota*, with an escort of four destroyers, *Walke, Benham, Preston* and *Gwin*. During the nights 14–15 November the Japanese 2nd Fleet (Vice-Admiral Kondo) was despatched to shell the US base at Henderson Field; this fleet consisted of battleship *Kirishima* and the heavy cruisers *Atago* and *Takao*, with two escort groups, one comprising cruiser *Negara* and five destroyers, the other cruiser *Sendai* and three destroyers.

By chance, these Japanese and American forces approached Iron Bottom Sound from opposite directions and met head-on in the narrow gap between Savo Island and Guadalcanal nicknamed "The Slot". Both had destroyers scouting ahead and when the *Sendai* group encountered the US destroyers there was a furious but short-lived engagement in which three US destroyers, *Benham, Preston* and *Walke*, were sunk and the other, *Gwin*, damaged, while only one Japanese destroyer was damaged. This left the bigger ships manoeuvring for advantage: on the Japanese side were *Kirishima* (eight 14in, 16 6in) and *Atago* and *Takao* (total 20 8in, eight 4.7in), opposed to two US battleships with a total of 18 16in and 40 5in between them. At first the advantage lay with the Japanese, who found *South Dakota* (whose radar was inoperative), illuminated it with searchlights and then hit it no fewer than 42 times, inflicting heavy damage, particularly to control and communications systems.

In their excitement, however, the Japanese had failed to realise that *Washington* was also present, which used its radar to manoeuvre to within 9,000yd (8,250m) from where it opened a devastating fire on *Kirishima*, which sank seven minutes later. *Washington*, which was undamaged, avoided a torpedo attack from the Japanese destroyers and then covered the *South Dakota's* withdrawal, which despite the damage was still fully capable of moving under its own steam.

This was a remarkable outcome and every credit is due to *Washington* and its crew. The fact is that *Kirishima*, no mean ship, was overwhelmed in seven minutes flat.

LEFT: *USS* Washington *(BB-56) escorts the carrier* USS Lexington *(CV16) en route to attack the Gilbert Islands on 20 November 1942, while a Douglas SBD Dauntless dive-bomber flies overhead. At Second Guadalcanal* Washington *engaged the Japanese battleship* Kirishima *and sank it in precisely seven minutes – an astonishing achievement.*

RIGHT: *The two ships of the Washington-class were fine battleships, although they were somewhat over-shadowed by the larger, faster and more glamorous Iowa-class which followed.*

BELOW: North Carolina *in April 1942. One of the two Kingfisher floatplanes is about to be launched from the starboard catapult.*

INDEX